Typographic Systems

Kimberly Elam

Princeton Architectural Press, New York

# DESIGN BRIEFS ||||||||||||||||| *ESSENTIAL TEXTS ON DESIGN*

Published by
Princeton Architectural Press
37 East Seventh Street
New York, New York 10003

For a free catalog of books, call 1.800.722.6657.
Visit our web site at www.papress.com.

Library of Congress Cataloging-in-Publication Data
Elam, Kimberly, 1951–
     Typographic systems / Kimberly Elam.
159 p. : ill. (some col.) ; 22 cm.
Includes index.
ISBN-13: 978-1-56898-687-6 (pbk. : alk. paper)
1. Graphic design (Typography) 2. Composition (Art)
3. Visual communication. I. Title.
Z246.E5345 2007
686.2'2–dc22
                                    2006031370

Book Design: Kimberly Elam
Editor: Jennifer N. Thompson
Cover Design: Kimberly Elam, Deb Wood

Special thanks to:
Nettie Aljian, Sara Bader, Dorothy Ball, Nicola Bednarek,
Janet Behning, Becca Casbon, Penny (Yuen Pik) Chu,
Russell Fernandez, Pete Fitzpatrick, Sara Hart, Jan Haux,
Clare Jacobson, John King, Mark Lamster, Nancy Eklund
Later, Linda Lee, Katharine Myers, Lauren Nelson Packard,
Jane Sheinman, Scott Tennent, Paul Wagner, Joseph
Weston, and Deb Wood of Princeton Architectural Press
—Kevin C. Lippert, publisher

# Contents

## Introduction

All design is based on a structural system. These systems or frameworks can be broken down into eight major variations with an infinite variety of compositions within each system. Once essential visual organization systems are understood, the designer can fluidly organize words or images within a structure, combination of structures, or create a variation of a structure. Typographic organization is complex because the elements are dependent on communication in order to function. Additional criteria such as hierarchy, order of reading, legibility, and contrast come into play.

The typographic systems are akin to what architects term *shape grammars*. Through shape grammars, styles are identified via rule-based compositional systems. These shape grammars are employed for both historic analysis of style and for design. The eight typographic systems are similar in that each system has a set of rules that is unique and provides a sense of purpose that focuses and directs the decision-making. The resulting design becomes a visual language based on the shape grammar. Curiously, it is this focus and the restraint of the system that encourages creativity as the designer explores composition.

Student designers at first find the systems strange and awkward because they rarely see them in print or screen communications. However, as work develops, an understanding of the system emerges that enables the creative potential of the system to be realized.

Many designers focus primarily on the traditional grid system for design and are unaware of the potential that other systems hold for the graphic designer. The visual examples illustrate a broad range of design solutions and give designers, educators, and students insight into expanding their knowledge of organizational approaches to typographic design well beyond the grid.

**Kimberly Elam**

**Ringling School of Art and Design**
Department of Graphic and Interactive Communication
Sarasota, Florida

## Project Elements and Process

An understanding of systems of visual organization gives the designer an in-depth knowledge of the design process. The traditional ties that bind design education and visual process to the rigid horizontal and vertical grid systems of letterpress are no longer the sole means of order and efficiency in production. It is possible for the designer to use a more fluid means to create typographic messages through the eight systems of typographic organization. These systems expand the visual language of typographic communication and invite the reader into the text.

The approach to a process-oriented exploration of systems of visual organization is focused and simple. The eight systems—axial, radial, dilatational, random, grid, transitional, modular, and bilateral—are described in the following chapters, and the

All examples are organized with the system example on the left; one size, one weight composition in the middle; and composition with nonobjective elements at right.

**Axial System**
All elements are organized either to the left or right of a single axis.

**Radial System**
All elements extend from a point of focus.

**Dilatational System**
All elements expand from a central point in a circular fashion.

designer is challenged to use each system in the development of a type message. In turn, systems are visually investigated in two ways. The first, a series of compositions constrained to one size and one weight of type, is an exercise to truly experiment with the system beyond the obvious solutions. The second is a series of compositions with the option to use nonobjective elements and changes in tone to enhance the communication of the message.

The same eight-line message is used in all of the compositions in order to focus attention on the variations in the visual organization system. Continuity of the message enables comparisons to be made readily between the systems and encourages both an appreciation of typographic nuance and the limitless range of visual exploration.

Random System
Elements appear to have no specific pattern or relationship.

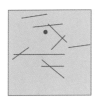 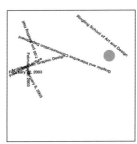 

Grid System
A system of vertical and horizontal divisions

Transitional System
An informal system of layered banding

## Project Elements and Process

Each of the systems has a distinct aesthetic and visual language. While most of the systems are inappropriate for lengthy messages, all of the systems can be crafted to communicate with a dynamic energy. The systems lend themselves best to interpretive communication, whereby the designer has considered the message tone, structure, length, and meaning. In this way the typography blends with the message to become an image, which becomes a dynamic invitation to the reader and one that enhances meaning.

Modular System
A series of non-objective elements that are constructed as standardized units

 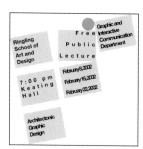 

Bilateral System
All text is arranged symmetrically on a single axis.

## Constraints and Options

Within any project process there are typographic constraints and options that provide opportunities for rich yet subtle variations. All lines of the message must be used in each composition. However, lines may be broken at will to change a single line into multiple lines, creating changes in grouping and the way in which the line is read. Leading is variable, which in turn creates changes in position and textures. Variable word spacing and letter spacing creates distinct changes in texture and tone.

**Line Breaks**
Lines may be broken at will to make multiple lines.

**Architectonic Graphic Design**

**Architectonic Graphic Design**

**Architectonic Graphic Design**

**Leading**
Leading can be tight to overlapping or wide and airy.

**Architectonic Graphic Design**

**Architectonic**

**Graphic**

**Design**

**Architectonic**

**Graphic**

**Design**

**Word and Letter Space**
Varying word spacing and letter spacing creates different textures. As letter spacing is increased, word spacing must also be increased in order to avoid confusion.

**Architectonic**

**Graphic Design**

**Architectonic**

**Graphic Design**

**Architectonic**

**Graphic Design**

## Constraints and Options

When the format is small and several of the line lengths are long, one of the first options is to break the lines. When lines are broken intuitively in a logical pattern, the result is a grouping of lines of text that belong together. Grouping is important as it simplifies the composition and enhances readability.

Initially, many designers are satisfied with the computer default values for leading, about 20% of the text size. As work continues, the designer should become sensitive to the texture of the text on the page and begin to investigate leading and experiment with dense and airy textures.

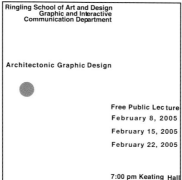

### Line Breaks
The longest line, "Graphic and Interactive Communication Department," must be broken in order to more fluidly compose the message (left). Once broken, the lines of text can be readily moved within the format (middle), and logically grouped (right).

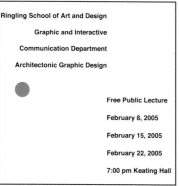
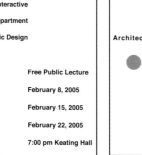
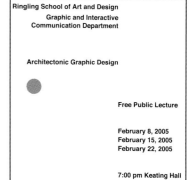

### Leading
During the beginning phases of the project, leading is often determined by the default values of the computer (left). As work progresses, the designer experiments with grouping lines of text and altering the leading between lines (middle). As sensitivity develops, the designer carefully plans and organizes leading, word spacing, and letter spacing (right).

## The Circle and Composition

The circle is a wildcard element, which means that it can be used anywhere in the composition. The circle, particularly in the restrained one size, one weight compositions, gives the designer a tool to guide the eye; create a pivot point, tension, and emphasis; or contribute to visual organization or balance.

In the one size, one weight series of compositions the placement of the circle can dramatically change the composition: squeezing the circle between lines of text can create tension; close proximity to a line or word can create emphasis; aligning the circle with lines gives a sense of organization;

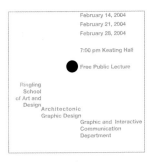

Emphasis Placement

Stopping Point Placement

Emphasis and Tension Placement

Organization Placement

Organization and Emphasis Placement

Emphasis Placement

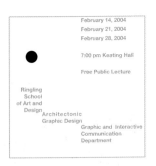

Balance Placement

Balance Placement and Pivot Point

Balance Placement and Pivot Point

placement in the upper left quadrant of the format often results in the creation of a starting point; and placement in the lower right quadrant results in a stopping point. When a designer finishes the thumbnail series of compositions, he or she is encouraged to develop yet another series with the strongest composition, moving only the circle. The next step is to evaluate the results. Within the series there are a number of very different but equally good choices. As a result, the designer realizes how a small element can completely change a composition and how it is read.

Emphasis and Organization Placement
The circle separates the two groups of text and emphasizes the white lines.

Tension Placement
The circle creates tension through proximity as the eye struggles to leave it and read the text.

Starting Point Placement
The circle floats into the black field and becomes the point where the eye enters the composition.

Stopping Point Placement
The circle activates the black space and becomes a stopping point for the eye.

## Nonobjective Elements

Using nonobjective elements sharpens and articulates the composition. Just as typography is functional in the communication of a message, the nonobjective elements enhance the functions of emphasis, organization, and balance. Nonobjective elements become functional guides when used with typography and communicate the message more clearly by enhancing a hierarchical order and directing the viewer's eye. In addition these elements can strengthen a message by communicating a sense of organization and direction. Designers have already been sensitized to the nuances of composition through the thumbnail and critique process; that same sensitivity is brought into play with nonobjective elements and tone. Designers usually find this phase of the project the most interesting and the results the most satisfying.

### Rule Series

Rules can both organize and emphasize a message. Single-weight rules of equal length function primarily as elements of organization. When there is a change in weight, the rules also create a rhythm and guide the eye downward. Altering the length of the rules creates a strong diagonal. Changes in rule weight create a hierarchy by guiding the eye to the largest volume of black.

Contemporary American Photographers

The Museum of Modern Art

June 12–15, 2001

Original Composition

Contemporary American Photographers

The Museum of Modern Art

June 12–15, 2001

Rules as Organizational Elements

### Circle Series

The circle can act as a nonobjective pivot point or as an element that creates hierarchy. The examples show ways in which the circle draws the eye to a single word, making that word the first read in the composition.

Contemporary American Photographers

The Museum of Modern Art

June 12–15, 2001

Contemporary American Photographers

The Museum of Modern Art

June 12–15, 2001

Circles that Create Emphasis and Hierarchy

### Tone Series

The simple use of tone can dramatically alter the hierarchy of a message. The eye is drawn to the largest volume of black on a white background or the largest volume of white on a black background. Words or portions of words can be emphasized, giving the message a sense of visual punctuation.

Contemporary American Photographers

The Museum of Modern Art

June 12–15, 2001

Contemporary American Photographers

The Museum of Modern Art

June 12–15, 2001

Tone Changes that Create Emphasis and Hierarchy

## Nonobjective Elements

The examples on this spread make use of simple nonobjective elements, such as rectangular strokes or rules, circles, and tone. In the rule series there are distinct visual differences between rules that are of consistent length and those that vary in length. When the widths vary, the visual arrangement is more complex. The circle, a visually compelling element, attracts attention no matter how small it is. Because of this the circle can readily be used as an element of emphasis. Finally, simple changes in tone can control hierarchy and the compositional texture of the message. In all of the examples the message does not change, but the way in which the message is read does.

The use of nonobjective elements should be carefully considered and caution must be taken to avoid using elements that overwhelm the message, either because of the volume of color or the complex shape.

Contemporary American Photographers

The Museum of Modern Art

June 12–15, 2001

Rules as Rhythmical Elements

Contemporary American Photographers

The Museum of Modern Art

June 12–15, 2001

Rules Emphasizing the Diagonal

Contemporary American Photographers

The Museum of Modern Art

June 12–15, 2001

Rules Emphasizing a Hierarchy

Contemporary American Photographers

The Museum of Modern Art

June 12–15, 2001

Contemporary American Photographers

The Museum of Modern Art

June 12–15, 2001

Contemporary American Photographers

The Museum of Modern Art

June 12–15, 2001

Contemporary American **Photographers**

The Museum of Modern **Art**

**June** 12–15, 2001

Contemporary **American** Photographers

The **Museum** of **Modern** Art

**June** 12–15, 2001

Contemporary American **Photographers**

The **Museum of Modern** Art

**June** 12–15, 2001

## 1. Axial System

**Design to the left and right of a single axis**

ARCHITECTONIC
GRAPHIC DESIGN

Ringling
School
of Art
and Design

Graphic and
Interactive
Communication
Department

Free
Public
Lecture

7:00 pm
Keating Hall

February 14, 2004
February 21, 2004
February 28, 2004

The axial system is one of the simplest systems. All elements are organized either to the left or right of a single axis. This is a branching arrangement from an implied main line. The axis can exist anywhere in the format to create a symmetric or asymmetric composition. Examples of axial arrangements in nature include the trunks of trees, flower stems, and many other plants.

Experience working with the axial system reveals that asymmetric arrangements are often more interesting than symmetrical ones. When the axis is placed off center to the left or right the space is divided in a more interesting way, with a shift in the proportion of larger and smaller volumes of space. The use of asymmetry results in a relatively simple visual arrangement with heightened visual interest.

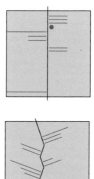

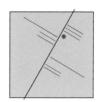

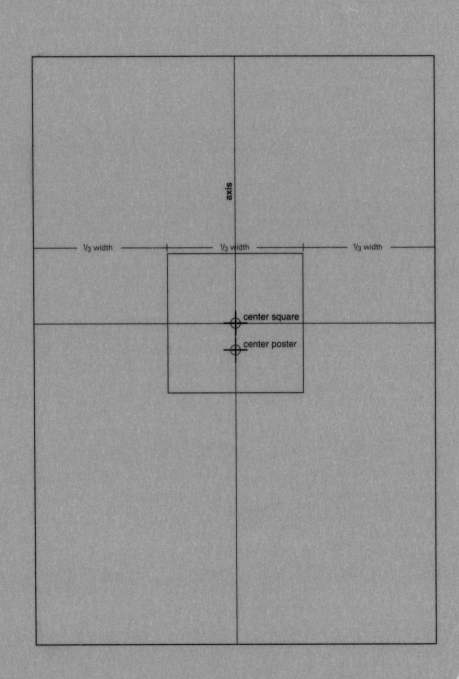

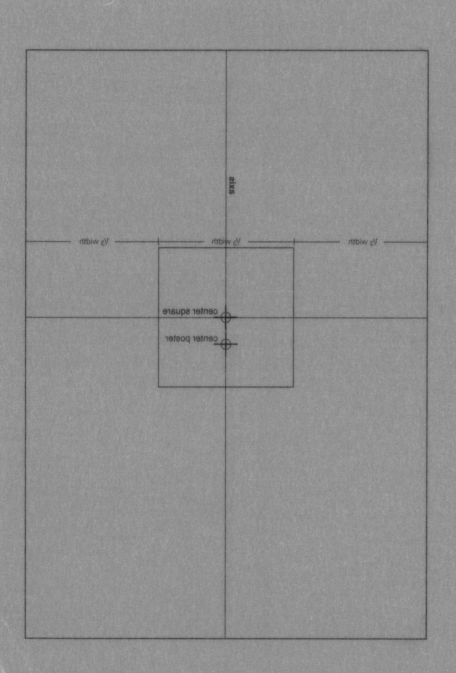

**Axial System**

While many axial system compositions benefit from asymmetric placement, this poster employs the symmetry of the centered axis to evoke and celebrate the simplicity of Le Corbusier's modern architecture. The single-axis typographic arrangement splits the poster and the glossy center square over the face. The photographic image provides asymmetric accent in the hand that lifts the architect's signature geometric glasses. Two fine white horizontal rules on the left and right edges imply a horizontal line that bisects the glossy square and focuses the viewer's eyes on the image.

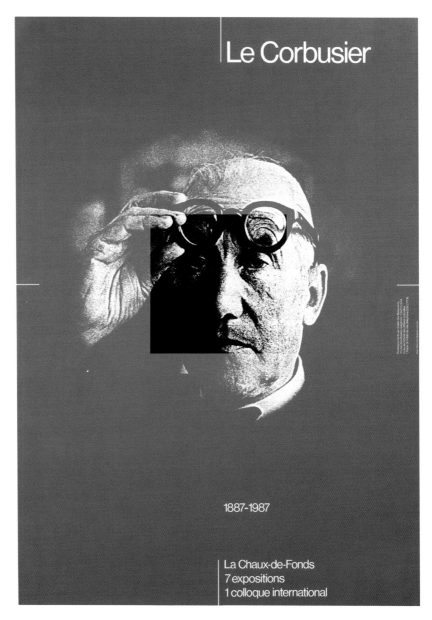

Werner Jerker, 1987

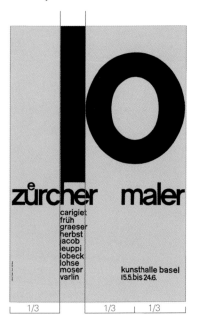

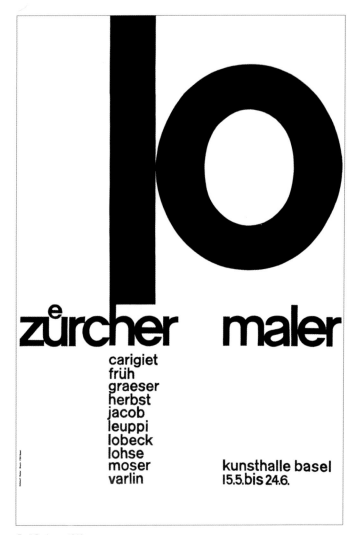

Dietmar Winkler uses a single curved axis to complete the shape of the bell of a horn in his poster for the program Music for Brass.

Emil Ruder, c. 1960

Emil Ruder's single-axis poster 10 zurcher maler (10 Zürich Artists) uses the strong vertical stress of the number 1. The emphasis on the vertical movement is increased because the stroke bleeds off of the top of the poster and is connected to the "h." The proportions of the poster are divided vertically by the 1 and column of names in a pleasing $1/3:2/3$ ratio.

Dietmar Winkler

## Wide Column Widths

Longer line lengths are less flexible but still provide potential for compositional interest. In the example to the right, a change in proportion of space occurs above and below the text. The composition experiments with the idea that the lines do not need to be horizontal or right side up. The slight angled variations from the baseline are visually unsettling, attract attention, and increase interest. The compositions below use a similar strategy and separate the groups of text with changes in tone. Both mass the text in a single location, allowing the expansive background space to modify it.

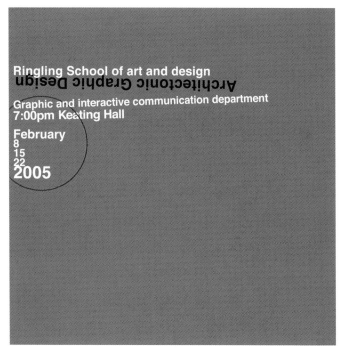

Jonathon Seniw

Study for the nonobjective composition to the right.

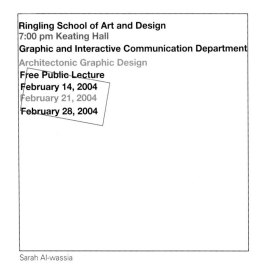

Sarah Al-wassia

Mona Bagla

## Transparency

Computers have given the designer desktop tools that were once only available to photographers and darkroom technicians. The interpretation of the nonobjective elements as transparent overlapping planes is an engaging idea. There is a rhythm to the planes and color change as the planes overlap and emphasize the axis.

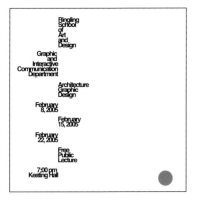

Study in one size, one weight for the non-objective composition to the right.

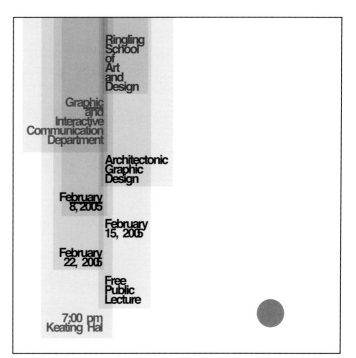

Nicholas Lafakis

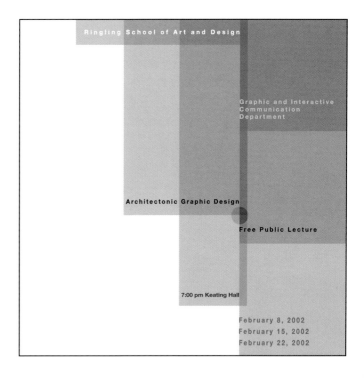

## Transparency

Nonobjective work only begins after the designer has experimented with composition using only one size and one weight of type. The examples below are from the initial one size, one weight thumbnail exercises and show the designer's process, developing a strong axial composition in preparation for working with nonobjective elements.

The work to the right is from the nonobjective series and is an example of how changes in tone and the introduction of transparent nonobjective elements can enhance a composition. The simple structure is modified by the introduction of two rectangles and a circle that highlights the presence of the corner. Groups of text are identified by changes in tone, and the two longest lines are modified by placement near the edges of the rectangles.

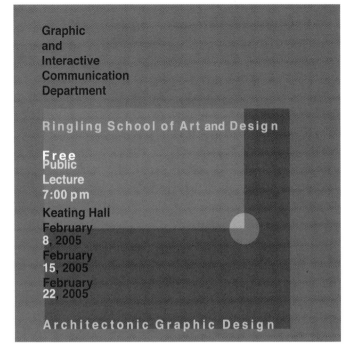

Kisa Brown

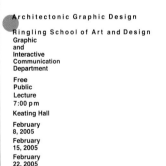

Part of a series of studies in one size, one weight for the nonobjective composition shown above.

## Horizontal Movement

Many axial compositions have a strong vertical movement due to alignment along a single axis. This composition (right) changes the visual stress through the use of horizontal rectangles that span the format and emphasize the title. All type elements strictly correspond to the axis, but the horizontal movement is so strong that they appear to float. Below are a series of thumbnails by the same designer that show the range of visual thinking within the project.

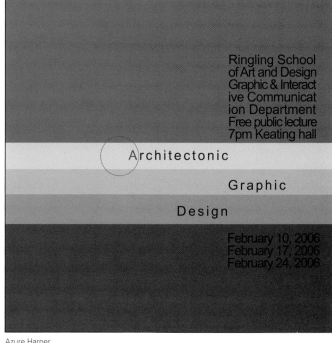

Azure Harper

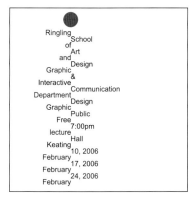

Part of a series of studies in one size, one weight for the nonobjective composition shown above.

Azure Harper

## Shaped Background

Nonobjective elements can expand to create a background that shapes the space. The shaped backgrounds in these works guide the eye as it follows the text and adds visual interest. Though the typographic compositions remain axial arrangements, they appear more lively.

In the composition to the right, the repeated and split circle provides contrast with the vertical axis. The widely tracked light gray text also contrasts with the tightly tracked text on the gray field.

Below left, the background space is divided with a step-stairs shape that echoes the shape created by the blocks of text. The background is divided into a large dark gray field and a much smaller lighter gray field.

Below right, the circle overlaps and contrasts with the interior gray shape that leads the eye to the axis and the text.

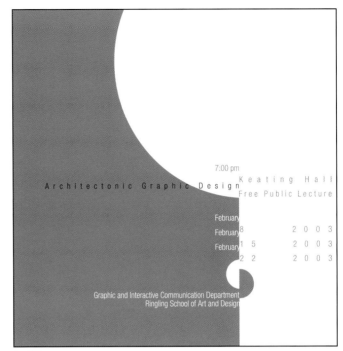

Loni Diep

Ann Marie Rapach

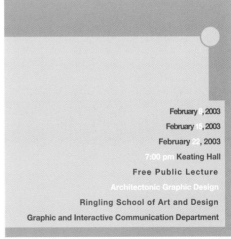

Dustin Blouse

## Implied Shaped Axis

An axis that is perpendicular to the baseline of the format is the most common arrangement, but the system also lends itself to the use of shaped axes. These shaped axes can include a single bend or many bends to create a zigzag effect. Grouping of the lines of text allows the composition to appear less complex and more cohesive and also crisply defines the shaped axis.

The axis (top) is implied and only defined by the edges of the blocks of text. The axis (bottom) is a much more complex zigzag that is also defined by the blocks of text. An implied axis is subtle and leaves much to the imagination.

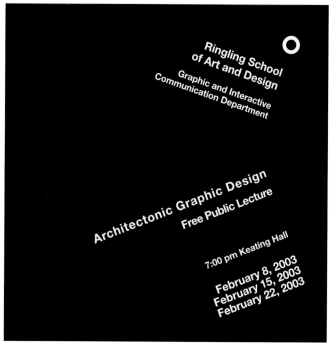

Jeremy Borthwick

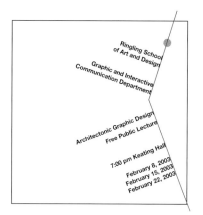

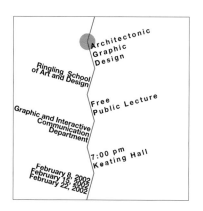

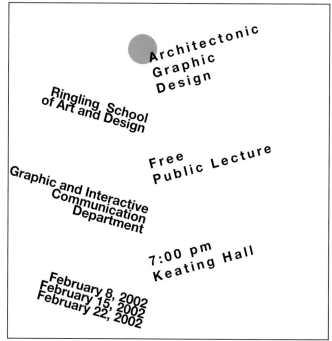

Melissa Rivenburgh

## Explicit Shaped Axis

The use of tone and nonobjective elements sharpens the composition by trapping color, dividing the space, and emphasizing the shape of the axis, resulting in compositions that are striking and visually forceful. Nonobjective elements can identify the shaped axis more clearly and divide the compositional space with line or a change in tone.

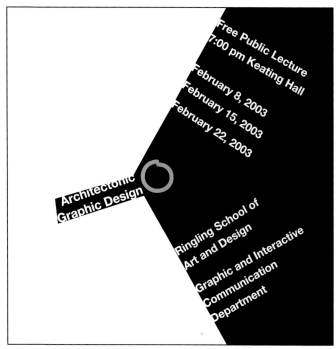

Rebekah Wilkins

Loni Diep

Rebekah Wilkins

## Diagonal Axis

Virtually any axial composition can be rotated on a diagonal. Since the diagonal is the most dynamic visual direction, the result is an active composition with implied movement. The compositional space becomes more complex because the negative space is divided into triangles rather than rectangles or squares.

The one size, one weight study below is the basis for the nonobjective composition to the right. The typographic composition is only slightly altered in the rotation to the diagonal. The black background and shaped gray field introduce an element that breaks up the space; the gray field is shaped to create divergency and emphasize the time of the presentation.

Loni Diep

Studies in one size, one weight for the nonobjective composition above.

## Diagonal Axis

The example to the right is an elegant play on diagonal composition. Similar to the Odermatt & Tissi poster in the professional work section of this chapter, the lines are placed on the diagonal and arranged on a vertical axis. There is a strong sense of movement as the viewer's eye moves toward the axis as each line is read. The geometric rectangle of black space to the right of the axis contrasts with the irregular space on the left. Changes in grouping, tone, and leading emphasize a hierarchy.

The works below employ a more traditional diagonal. Both use changes in tone to separate lines and groups of text. The scale of the text below left is large and easy to read, and the red rule modifies and emphasizes the department name and the title of the lecture. The scale of the text below right is smaller and the composition is much more compact. The result is that the changes in the tone are subtle, making it more difficult to read, but also more intriguing.

Kieshea Edwards

Melissa Pena

Mona Bagla

## 2. Radial System

**Design from a central point of focus**

In the radial system all elements are organized to extend from a central point of focus like rays. Examples include the petals of flowers, fireworks, domes in architecture, rays of the sun, spokes of a wheel, starfish, etc. The compositions are dynamic, as the eye is drawn to the focal point of the radial composition. This point can be implied or depicted.

Depending on the orientation of the lines, readability of the message may be diminished as the type leaves the traditional horizontal baseline. Within this system lines of text can be arranged to read in a number of different ways: top to bottom, bottom to top, right side up, or upside down. In order to create a functional message, the lines of text should be arranged in the most comfortable manner possible.

Most examples of radial structure are highly symmetrical, such as flowers, architectural domes, and starfish. Because the rays create a circle, the forms are visually very satisfying. When working with text, the resulting compositions often contain portions of a single circle or many circles. The resulting asymmetry is less satisfying and more visually interesting.

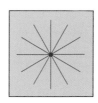

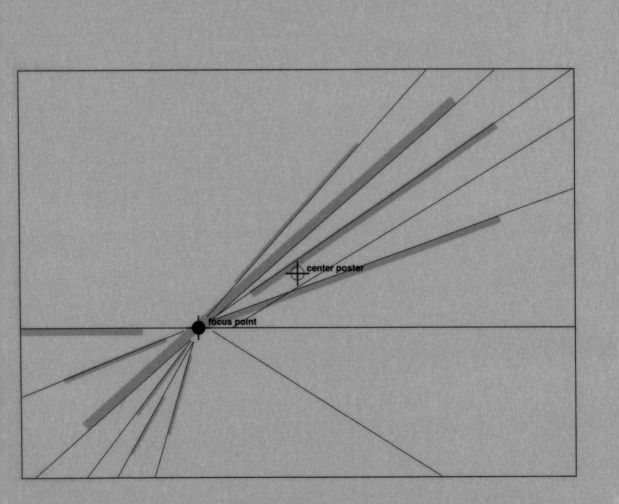

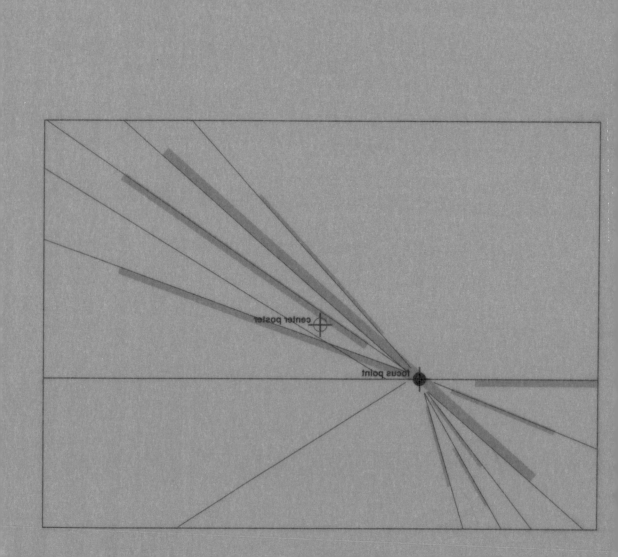

# Radial System

In the Old Truman Brewery poster the radial system is used to communicate the transformation of an industrial warehouse to "a centre for young design talent so sharp it could cut diamonds." The text is arranged around a center focus point and a strong horizontal line, and sharp angles of text slice the collaged images in dynamic pinwheel fashion.

The radial system becomes the foil for communicating the dynamic intent that is focused on the building. Lines of text move toward the center point and then radiate out as a fitting tribute to the design talent housed within and the effect they will have on the community.

Paul Humphrey and Luke Davies, Insect, 1998

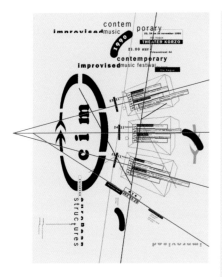

*Bring in Da Noise, Bring in Da Funk* is a musical that celebrates characters through tap dancing and music. The sole of a tap shoe is the focal point for type that radiates from it. The result is an informal composition made all the more spontaneous by irregularities and changes in the handwritten type. Text is separated by hand-drawn rules and the radial aspects are intensified by the size change for the words "NOISE" and "FUNK."

Paula Scher, Pentagram Design, 1996

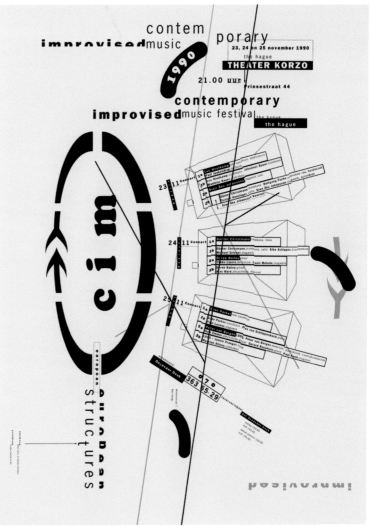

Allen Hori, Studio Dumbar, 1990

The visual arrangement for the Contemporary Improvised Music Festival poster is a play in two- and three-dimensional space. Blocks of text on dimensional shapes radiate around an ellipse. Text is organized by date in outlined rectangular shapes and emphasized by dropped-out black rectangles.

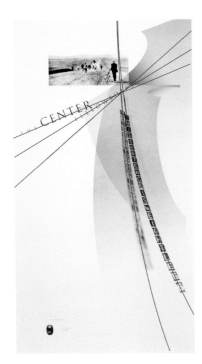

The feeling of space and movement is effortlessly captured by Rebeca Mendez in this poster for The Getty Center Fellowships. The eye is drawn to a sepia photograph of travelers moving toward a point in the distance. The arc of text, "this sentence is weightless" floats in the breeze and guides the eye to the focal point.

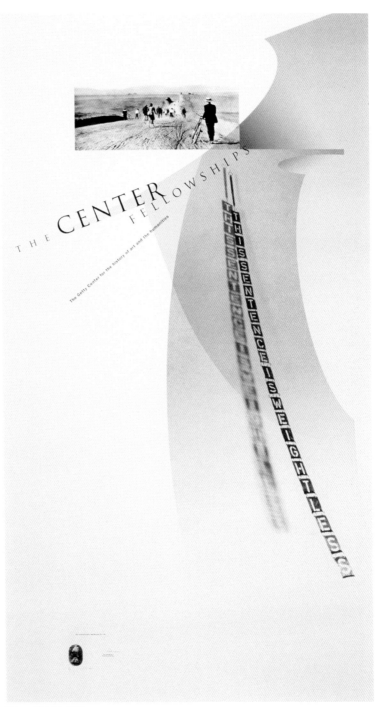

Rebeca Mendez, 1995

The radial system immediately presents a compositional challenge because each line most readily exists as an individual unit with a relationship only to the focal point. Many initial compositions often resemble a star burst with evenly spaced elements. These compositions appear complex because the lines have not been grouped and the negative spaces are similarly sized pie wedges. As work progresses the placement of the focal point changes to asymmetric off-center positions or locations off the page, and there is an increasing sensitivity to white space. Further experience with the system often yields interesting groupings of lines, simplified compositions, and more dense textures. Because of the

**Initial Phase**
Initially, radial components occupy a considerable amount of compositional space, because each line is seen as an individual element.

**Intermediate Phase**
Once the designer is comfortable with the radial system, experimentation begins with curved lines, arranging space between lines, grouping lines, grouping and right-angle arrangements, and corner focal point placement.

**Advanced Phase**
As further experience with the radial system develops, designers focus on grouping lines of text and creating a hierarchy. The focal point can be reinterpreted from an imagined pin point to the implied center of a large circle. Alignment of the lines and arrangement at right angles yields a more formal and inventive result. Placing an implied focal point outside the page permits the lines to be arranged at slight angles.

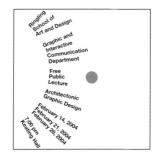
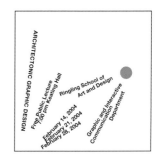

strong diagonal direction inherent in radial compositions, they are visually active and dynamic. Clearly, however, radial compositions are difficult to read and are most appropriate for visual messages with limited amounts of text.

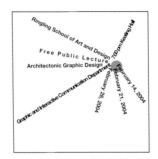

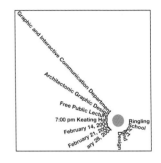

## Emphasis Strategies

The composition is the same in all three works on this page, with text separated into groups and then rotated to separate the groups with space. Changes in color and tone and different versions of the circle bring variety. The color red is used sparingly as an emphasis accent. The offset circle is used as a unifying element (right), as an element of emphasis (below left), and finally, only implied (below right).

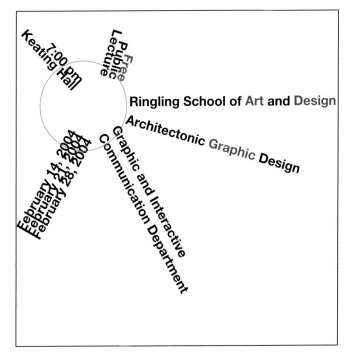

Andrea Cannistra

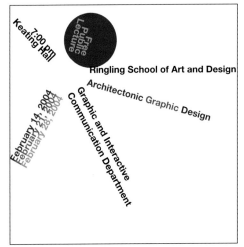

Andrea Cannistra

Andrea Cannistra

## Grouping Strategies

Within the radial system it is difficult to create a clear hierarchy because the lines most comfortably stand alone. These compositions allow lines to radiate as individuals and consciously use changes in tone, color, and nonobjective elements to create a hierarchy to guide the reader. Three strategies are employed to create order. The first strategy (right) uses the nonobjective element of the black arc, which becomes a ground for the text. The text in the black field is read first (1), then the red text (2), the date (3), and finally the gray text (4). The second strategy (below left) uses rectangles that merge into a single shape and group the text. The third strategy (below right) groups text through changes in color and tone.

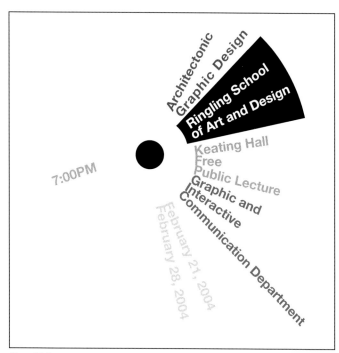

Chean Wei Law

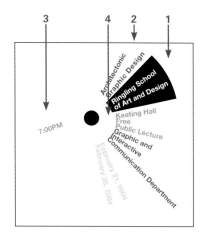

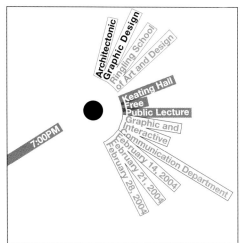

Chean Wei Law

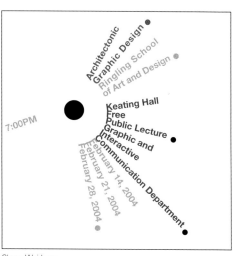

Chean Wei Law

## Rules and Hierarchy

Careful use of tone and nonobjective elements enhances these works. The larger example (right) successfully uses rules to guide the reader to the most important text. The manner in which the white text bleeds off of the edge of the rules adds further visual interest, as does the red text. The small gray background composition (bottom left) employs a change in tone and a change in case to create a hierarchy, but the result is very active and confusing. In the third composition (below right) an even simpler strategy is used; the gray triangular field emphasizes the title of the lecture and divides the page into three proportional areas.

Jeremy Cox

Jeremy Cox

Jeremy Cox

## Transparent Radial Planes

Attaching the lines of text to a transparent rectangular plane and rotating the plane yields striking results. The overlapping planes intensify the radial directional movement—not toward the center point, but around the center point—and the planes create additional shapes as they overlap. The type in the composition to the right attaches itself to the plane and also becomes part of the background as it bleeds off of the edge. Both the plane and the text are affected by the transparency. The movement is even stronger below because the rotate and repeat pattern corners guide the eye, and the tone in the text changes from a darker to a lighter gray.

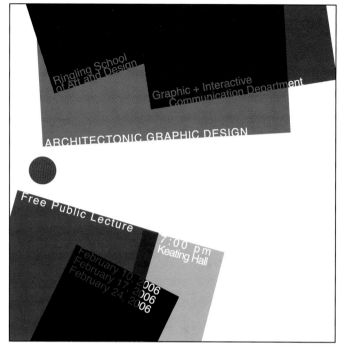

Willie Diaz

Study in one size, one weight for the nonobjective composition to the right.

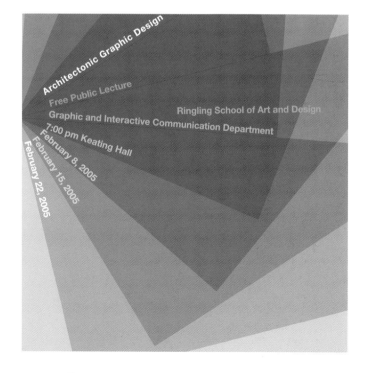

## Enclosure

The use of a shape enclosure in a radial composition can aid in simplifying
the composition. In the composition
to the right the white rectangle that
moves into the format encloses the
title and divides the background space
in an unexpected way. Hairline arcs
in the composition below divide the
space into two areas and two groups.
The larger group is subdivided with a
dashed line that emphasizes the title
and creates a subordinate arc.

Casey Diehl

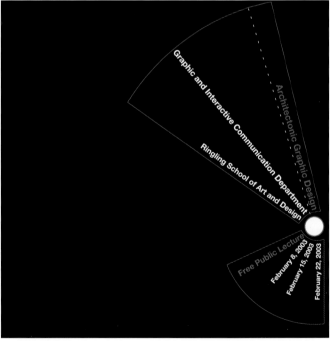

Ian Hoene

## Circle Alignment

The consistent arrangement of text in these works and the use of tone rather than additional nonobjective elements enhances readability. In both of these works the lines of text radiate along an implied circle, and the simplicity of the composition, as well as the clearly defined grouping, enhances readability. Tone change (right) and the use of red in the title further define groups and create a hierarchy. The use of a single line on an arc (below) serves to create diversity within the unified structure and make that line first in reading order.

Mike Plymale

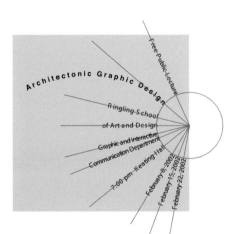

Study in structure and one size, one weight for the nonobjective composition shown on the right.

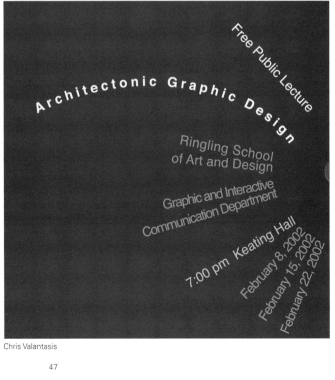

Chris Valantasis

## Right and Obtuse Angles

The works on this spread interpret the radial system with lines that radiate at right angles (90°) or obtuse angles, (90–120°). The text is grouped and placed at an angle to achieve a very controlled and distinctly different result from most radial compositions. The interrelationships of the lines are more formal, intentional, and often easier to read. The negative space is also clearly divided into rectangles or triangles that are pleasing.

The right angle composition (right) is articulated by the square focal point. The text is divided into four groups, and each group relates to an edge of the square. Repetition of white text in the background creates a texture, and the change in text weight and red accent emphasize the most important elements of the message. The obtuse angle composition (below) is divided into angles of 120° that proportionally divide the background. The most important group is emphasized with a black, shaped rule.

Jose Rodriguez

Early study for the nonobjective composition to the right.

Forrest Moulton

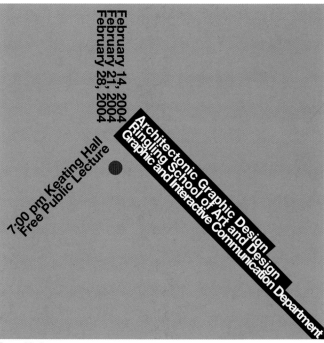

Forrest Moulton

## Right Angles

The use of the tone can crisply divide the format into distinct areas. In the composition to the right, the gray text in the black field attaches to and bleeds into the gray field, as does the black text in the gray field, which solidifies the position of the text. The visually satisfying single line of text in white is given a sense of movement by the thin black rule, and it seems to invade the space.

The composition below left is compellingly simple. The text is arranged in three groups at right angles to the circle. The flush alignment of the text creates the implied edges of a square, and the background space is separated into two rectangles with pleasing proportions.

Because the format is diagonal and is divided into four triangles, the composition shown below right is complex. The complexity is increased as the tone of the top dark gray triangle extends into two rectangles that define the other triangles. Groups of text merge at the focal point, creating tension.

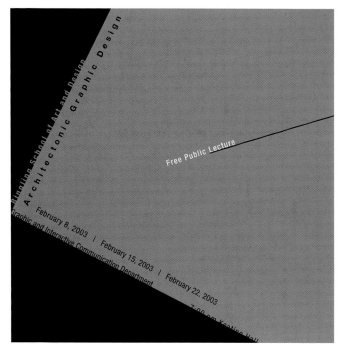

Loni Diep

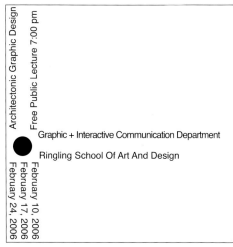

Elizabeth van Kleef

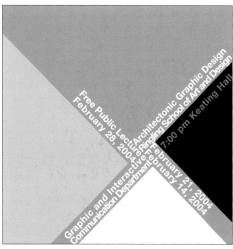

Nathan Russell Hardy

## Spiral

The idea of placing text on a spiral is interesting, but problematic, as the lines turn upside down as they move around the curve. Here, the designer has enhanced the visual interpretation of the spiral by adjusting line length where possible and placing the two most important lines in the message, "Architectonic Graphic Design" and "Free Public Lecture" in the most comfortable position for reading.

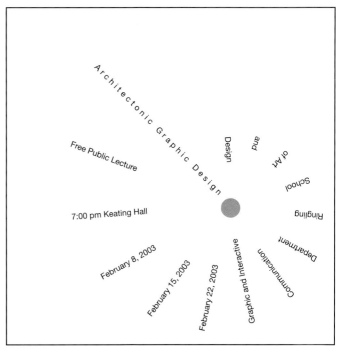

Loni Diep

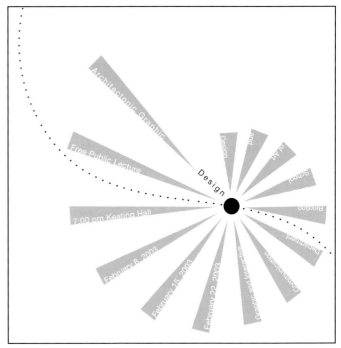

Loni Diep

## Enlarged Circle

The use of the greatly enlarged circle in the composition to the right plays on the idea of lines radiating from a point—in this case, the implied center of the circle. The huge circle is visually arresting and changes in case and text size create a hierarchy. In the composition below, the gray circle becomes a ground for the black lines of text. The focal point is far outside the format, and the lines gently radiate within the circle. The word "Design" falls outside the circle and is dropped out in white for emphasis.

Gray West

Rebekah Wilkins

## 3. Dilatational System

**Design along a circular path**

# Dilatational System, Introduction

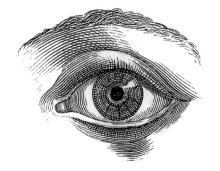

In a dilatational system circles dilate or expand from a central point. Examples of this system include the iris of the eye, the waves created when a pebble is dropped into still water, and sound waves. Similar to the radial system, the compositions are dynamic as the eye moves along the arc of the circle or is drawn to the focal point at the center of the circle.

The simplest forms of the dilatational system are circles that expand in regular or rhythmical increments from the center. Variations of this system can include dilations that are tangent, dilations that are non-concentric, and multiple dilations.

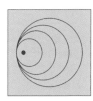

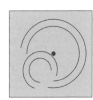

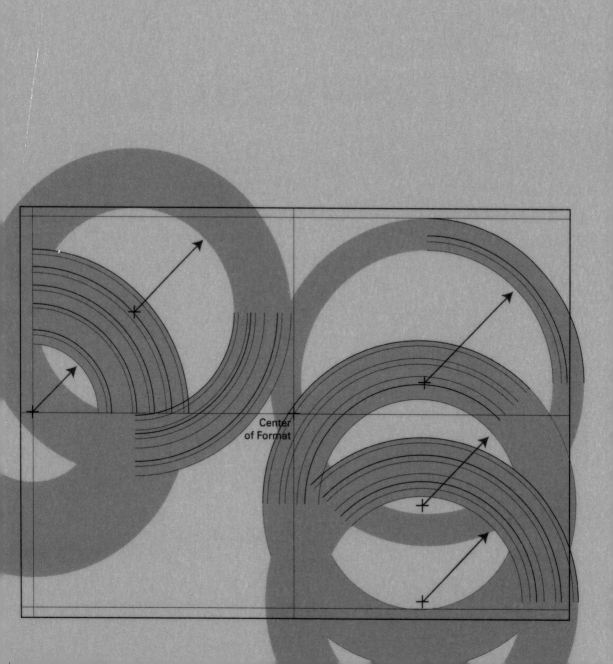

Center
of Format

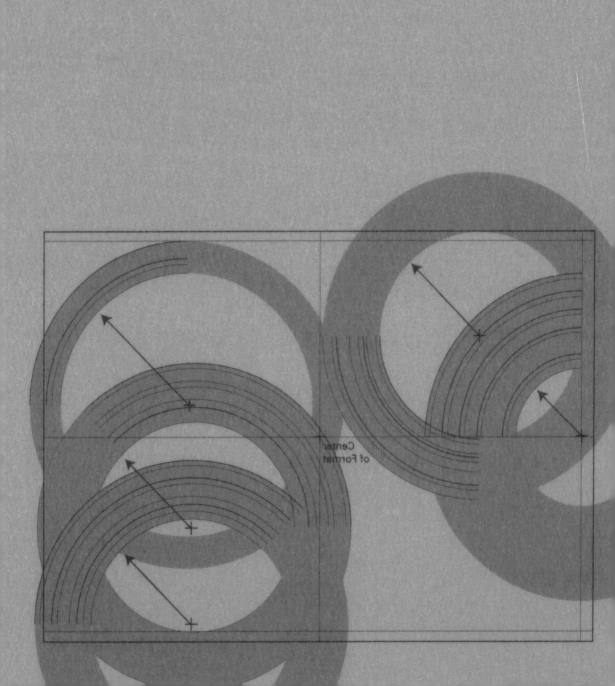

Center
of Format

## Dilatational System

Perhaps the dilatational movement of sound waves was the inspiration for the Experimental Music program cover series by Bernard Stein and Nicolaus Ott. All of the covers were designed for a contemporary music festival in conjunction with a fine arts academy and works included electronic music, computer music, and works that involved the combination of sound, light, and movement. The covers span an eight-year period of time, from 1982 to 1990, and variations of the dilatational structure became the visual language for six of the covers.

The economy of means in such a simple work is incredible. All of the covers double as both a folded program cover and a poster for the event. Two print colors are used on white stock, resulting in an economical print job. Only two sizes of text and three weights are used in a beautifully controlled hierarchal system. The table below details the order of text and the hierarchal system of scale, weight, color, and case employed by the designers.

**Hierarchal Order**

| Text | Scale | Weight | Color | Case |
| --- | --- | --- | --- | --- |
| Title 1, Month, Day: | Large | Bold | White | Uppercase |
| Weekday, Location, Year: | Small | Light | White | Upper & Lowercase |
| | | | | |
| Title 2, Surnames: | Large | Bold | Black | Uppercase |
| First Names, Selection: | Small | Light | Black | Upper & Lowercase |
| | | | | |
| Sponsor Credits: | Small | Medium | Black | Upper & Lowercase |

Bernard Stein and Nicolaus Ott, 1982

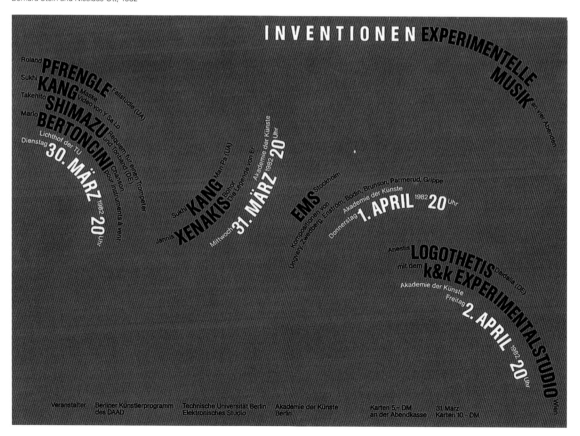

55

The text moves lyrically in concentric and intersecting circles across the front to the back of the covers. The dilatational system becomes the structure for the placement of groups of text and similar sized circles are used in all of the groups. The hierarchal system is carefully controlled in each of the groups. The surname of each of the artists appears in large bold black text. First names and other ancillary information is in smaller lightweight black text that aligns to the cap height. The dates and times of the performances appear in large bold white text, and again additional information appears in smaller lightweight white text. The systematic use of the dilatational movement and hierarchical order creates a composition that is both highly functional and quite beautiful.

The Inventionen '96 poster/cover (opposite, top) works with a series of similarly sized circles that are rotated from a single point. The hierarchical order is a simplified version of the earlier works, with the first and surnames of the artists in all lowercase white, the dates in all lowercase black. Each group consists of three lines organized concentrically, with the inner circle slightly offset. It is the offset inner circle that intensifies the sense of dynamic movement.

The Inventionen '83 poster/cover (opposite, bottom) is strongly directional. All of the arcs move toward an area of tension at the right. Although the width of the arcs varies due to the number of lines in each group, they are all similar as seen in the dark gray arcs. The hierarchy is similar to the earlier works, with surnames in large uppercase black, first names and music titles in small upper and lowercase black, days of the week in large uppercase white, and months in small uppercase white.

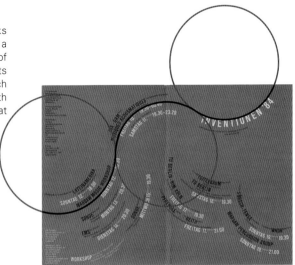

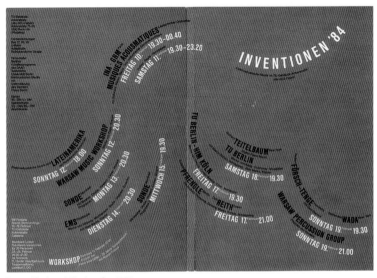

Bernard Stein and Nicolaus Ott, 1984

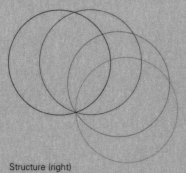

Structure (right)
Circles rotate from a pivot point.

Structure (below)
Arcs move in a similar direction toward
convergence. The left arc moves in a
different direction due to the interruption in
the sequence of program dates between
the 5th and the 7th.

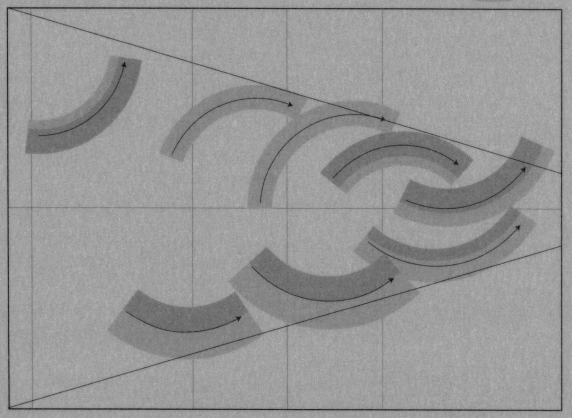

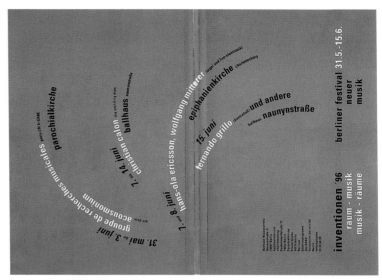

Bernard Stein and Nicolaus Ott, 1996

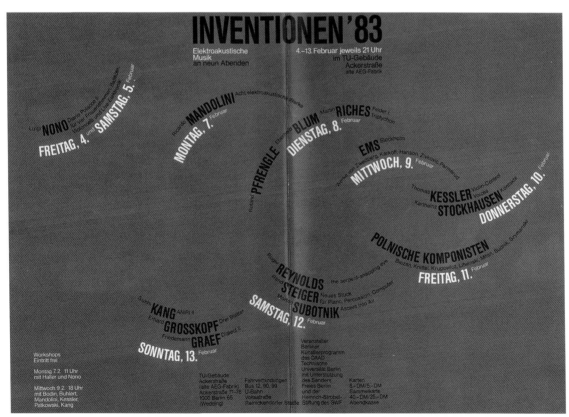

Bernard Stein and Nicolaus Ott, 1983

## Dilatational System, Thumbnail Variations

Even short visual messages are difficult to control in the dilatational system. The visual message used in all of the examples contains only eight lines of text, which is concise for investigational purposes. Text that is arranged in the dilatational system can easily be turned upside down or placed in an awkward position for reading. The designer needs to be constantly aware of reading comfort during composition.

This expansion from a central point creates implied dynamic forces as the eye seeks this point. In addition the visual forces not only dilate outward but also have a sense of rotational direction around the center. This is a double dynamic of implied outward expansion and rotation. Compositions can readily become complex and grouping of elements is often needed to simplify the message and consolidate visual forces.

### Initial Phase

Initial Investigations with the dilatational system involve acclimation to the unfamiliar positions of text on circular paths. Work tends to be experimental and unusual compositional textures and spaces are explored.

### Intermediate Phase

As the designer becomes familiar with the system, work begins to focus on grouping lines of text and organization.

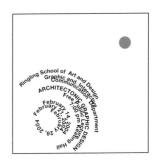

### Advanced Phase

With experience, compositional control is achieved, and the designer consciously groups lines and arranges space. Alignments are created and compositions are more orderly and simplified. Experiments investigate multiple dilatational groups and relationships between groups.

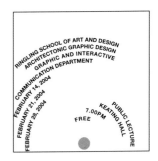

## Dilatational System, Thumbnail Variations

The most readable dilatational compositions bring a sense of order to the text through composition. Use of alignment can create order through interior axes in a composition. A step-stairs arrangement can guide the eye through rhythm and repetition. Grouping arcs of text can simplify compositions.

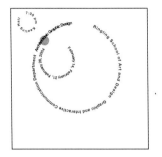

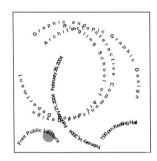

## Structure

Dilatational compositions change as the arrangement of the circles changes. The symmetrical composition at the top is similar to the bilateral system in that all elements are evenly arranged on a single centered axis. Allowing the circles to touch (below) yields a very different composition as lines of text move toward the tangent point. The resulting composition has characteristics of both the dilatational and the radial systems.

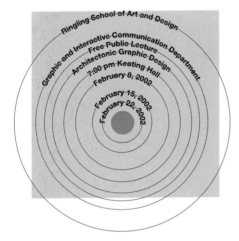

Omar Mendez

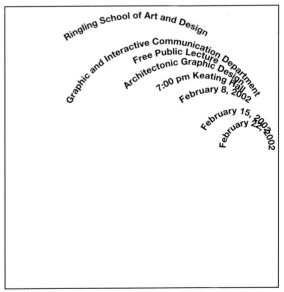

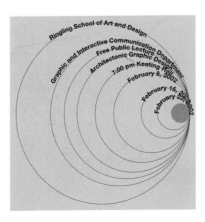

Omar Mendez

# Dilatational System

## Structure

Both compositions on this page group lines of text and employ a concentric step-stairs arrangement. The lines of text are rotated in increments to enhance a sense of movement. Asymmetry is emphasized in the bottom composition as the center of the circles is moved to the lower right.

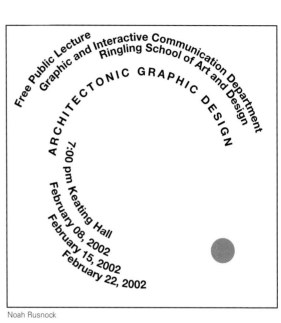

Noah Rusnock

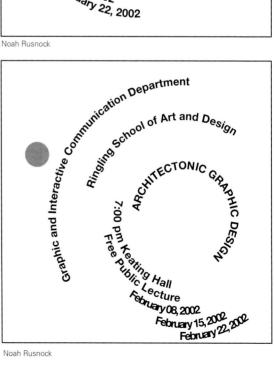

Noah Rusnock

## Nonobjective Elements

This composition is complex and captivating. The initial even increment arrangement is modified with circles that move near each other at an angle and rotate. The dense texture of the text is broken up by the further rotation of the smallest circles, which hold the dates. Nonobjective gray arcs, which become a ground for the text, enhance the composition through emphasis. The gray circle element follows the inventive pattern of the arcs as it is altered and split.

Gray West

# Dilatational System

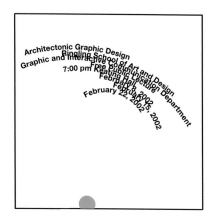

Gray West

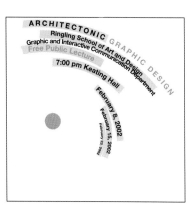

Gray West

Early studies for the nonobjective composition
shown opposite.

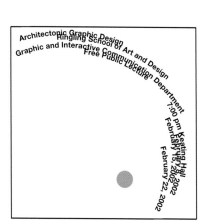

# Dilatational System

## Axis

The introduction of a strong axis makes this work a hybrid of both the axial and dilatational systems. The axis organizes the text by allowing the lines to relate to each other along the vertical line. In the work at the bottom the axes are near the edges of the format and perform a similar function.

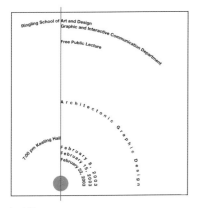

Loni Diep

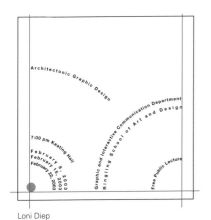

Loni Diep

Loni Diep

# Dilatational System

## Axis

A strong structure consisting of four tangent circles is the theme for these compositions. An axis that runs through the center of the format brings order and creates a point of alignment for the three interior lines. Here, the designer used red lines to explore three different methods of emphasizing the structure and guiding the eye. Enclosure (right) through a shaped outline arc emphasizes the axis. Circular movement (below left) is emphasized as the eye follows the spiral-like line. The axis (below right) is depicted by a vertical line.

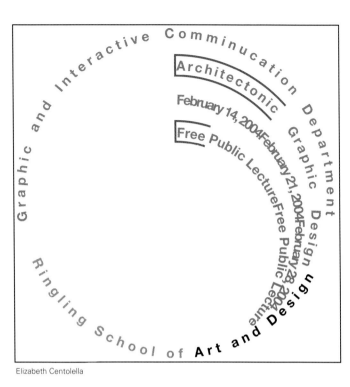

Elizabeth Centolella

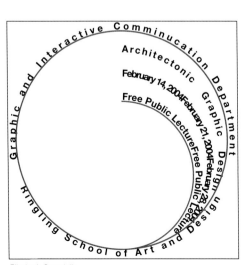

Elizabeth Centolella

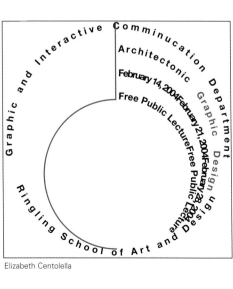

Elizabeth Centolella

## Spiral

The movement of the spiral is closely related to the dilatational system, and its use yields mixed results. Inevitably, some of the text appears upside down as it moves along the curve. Legibility is diminished as the eye follows the curve and struggles to read the message. The problems with legibility are offset by the visual interest created by the spiral line that winds around a fixed center point.

One size, one weight compositions (below) emphasize movement much more than the message. The background circles in the composition to the right do not serve to separate and identify lines of text as well as the change in tone shown in the example below on the right.

Elsa Chaves

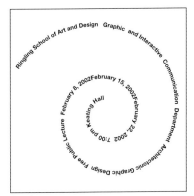

Chad Sawyer

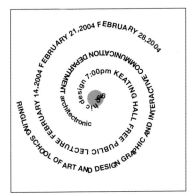

Nathan Russell Hardy

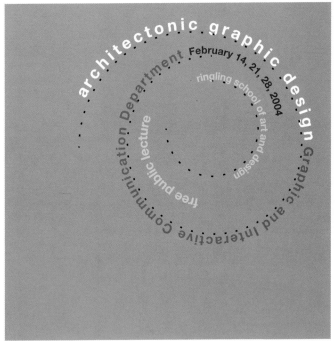

Elsa Chaves

## Double Spiral

In this example, the designer minimized the amount of upside-down text by using two spirals that move toward a point. A flush-left arrangement of the dates and fragmented words extends out from the spiral. The final composition is made all the more engaging as the spiral interrupts and changes the shape of the upper left corner and the lower right corner is cropped by the accent circle.

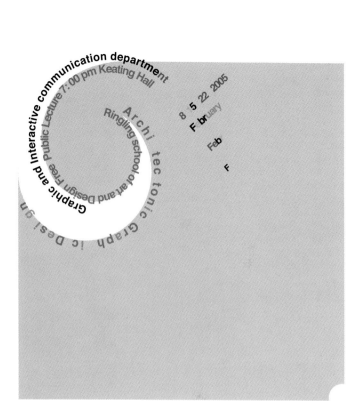

Eva Bodok

Early studies for the composition above.

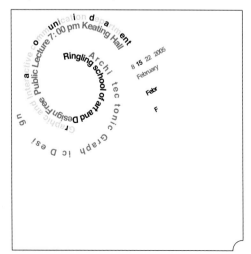

Eva Bodok

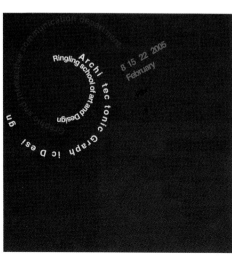

Eva Bodok

## Dilatational System

### Curvilinear

Introduction of tangent circles that create a curvilinear line is an inventive interpretation of the dilatational system. In the composition on the right, the eye starts reading the text in the lower left corner and sweeps up and around as one implied circle meets another. The text is split into two groups each arranged on a series of circles; the two groups are then related in a single curvilinear arc that unifies the composition. Multiple curves (bottom) are difficult to control and also need considerable space, resulting in type that is very small and compositions that are complex.

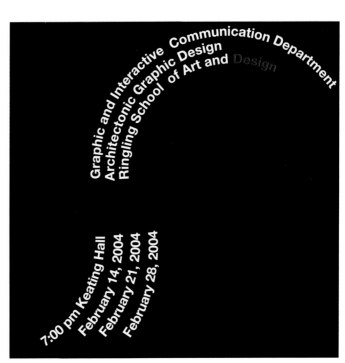

Mike Plymale

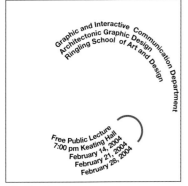

Mike Plymale

Early study for the composition to the right.

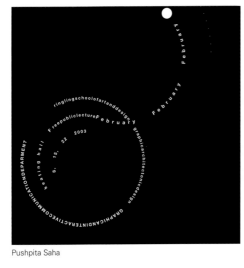

Pushpita Saha

Anthony Orsa

68

## Dilatational System

### Full Circles

Two overlapping circles are the visual theme for this series of compositions. The text has two groups—the larger circle holding the title, school, and department names, and the smaller circle, the dates. Changes in tone are used in all three compositions to indicate changes in the information. Below right, for example, the title is red and the school and department are white. In the large composition to the right multiple fine lines are used behind the large circle to enhance the sense of movement. The restrained use of two circles that move away from the active repeated group add contrast and compositional unity.

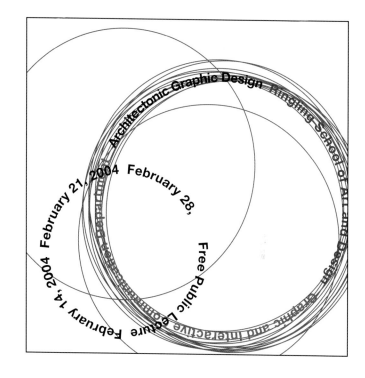

Heidi Dyer

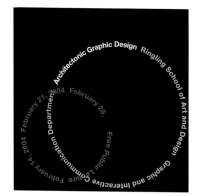

Heidi Dyer

Early study for the compositions.

Heidi Dyer

## 4. Random System

**Spontaneous design**

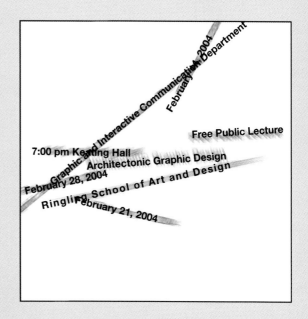

The random system consists of elements that are arranged without definite aim, pattern, direction, rule, method or purpose, but it is deceptively simple because the viewer imposes organization on compositions even when it is unintentional. The human eye and brain are keenly programmed to be pattern-seeking, image-seeking, and order-seeking because these abilities insured survival in early man. For centuries humans have found images in the constellations of stars in the sky or in cloud formations.

Work is often begun by scattering elements in the compositional field with free abandon. Inevitably, some of those elements align and the composition feels intentional. Success is more frequent when legibility diminishes with cropping, overlapping, and placing text at odd angles, which are cues of randomness. Surprisingly, random placement often yields a very dynamic and spontaneous result that, although difficult to read, is visually satisfying.

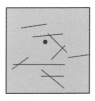

Random Traits
Although there are no rules for the random system, experimentation with the goal of achieving randomness quickly results in the discovery of a series of traits that are visual cues. Random elements are often:

overlapped
cropped
angled
textured
not horizontal
not aligned
not patterned

**Random System**

The Ba-Tsu 1994 poster is immediately arresting and is as intriguing as the designer himself. The poster is for a fashion retailer and entirely lacks the expected image of the product. The only clue to the purpose of the poster are the company name, date, and location. The type appears haphazard and is collaged in three-dimensional space. There are no alignments and the visual relationships that can be found are disrupted as each individual letter form moves and tilts randomly in space. A few selected characters highlighted with color break up the texture of gray and black. The result is an indiscriminate composition of type that is also remarkably cohesive.

Makoto Saito has stated, "I follow the instincts of my senses or my imagination." His approach to his work rests within the nexus of graphic design and fine art. He defies tradition by approaching each project with fresh artistic expression.

Makoto Saito, 1994

Makoto Saito, 1994

Another poster for Ba-Tsu employs the dynamic visual energy of the fluctuating dimensional letter forms. An enigmatic space is created by the cropped images and typography, which floats and moves in space.

David Carson, 1997

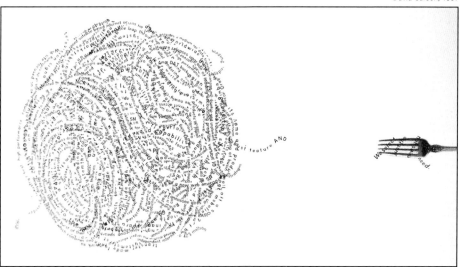

Gail Swanlund, Swank Design, 1994

In Gail Swanlund's "Life's A Dream" poster there is a mysterious dream-like quality of collaged text and images. Type elements are freely composed, loosely related, and altered with the addition of extra lines and abstract wings.

David Carson, 1997

David Carson's ads for an internet search company play on the idea of finding what is needed from random chaos. The fork (left) spears just the right text from the spaghetti and the fly paper captures "the news you need."

When lines of text are on the horizontal it is almost impossible to achieve a random effect. Any single direction—horizontal, vertical, or diagonal—indicates a sense of order and intention. Multiple angles immediately impart a sense of randomness and the more dramatic and varied the angles, the stronger the random sense.

Overlapping and cropping are natural occurrences in compositions with multiple angles and are some of the strongest random cues. Intentional typographic composition designed to communicate rarely overlaps or is cropped because readability is often inhibited.

### Initial Phase

Designers quickly discover that leaving the lines of text on a horizontal baseline or only slightly angled does not fully communicate randomness. In many of the compositions there is little tension because of the space surrounding the lines and an even texture throughout.

### Intermediate Phase

As work progresses experiments begin with multiple angles and overlapping lines. The angles become more dramatic as the designer grows more comfortable with overlapping lines, which reduces legibility. The designer also becomes sensitized to composition and the shapes and position of white space.

### Advanced Phase

During this phase the designer pushes the sense of randomness to illegibility through repetition, breaking the lines to individual words and, finally, to compositions of individual characters.

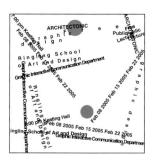

Texture variation also assists in the creation of random compositions. Evenly spaced type with default tracking produces an ordinary readable texture. Variation in the textures of type sometimes to the extreme communicate a change in the ordinary. It is valuable in this system to make the composition abstract by regarding the lines of text as texture only, and not as elements of communication. As texture the lines of text become important compositionally in terms of the shapes and negative space they create.

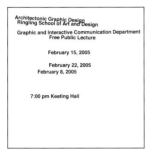

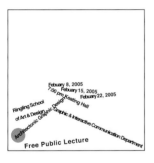
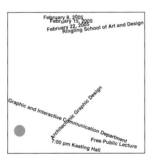

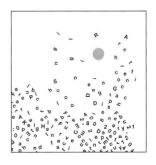

## Type Only

Admittedly, with random system compositions, readability of the message is often greatly diminished, which calls into question its utility as a method of communication. However, with some struggle, many of the compositions can be deciphered, and the spontaneous explosion of typography is distinctly appealing.

The purpose of working with the random system is experimentation, and within that process there are differing levels of readability. Most designers begin with relatively legible work, like the composition to the right, and move toward far less legible, like that shown below. The same is true of the works on the facing page. The smaller compositions are early, more legible works and the larger compositions are later, less legible works.

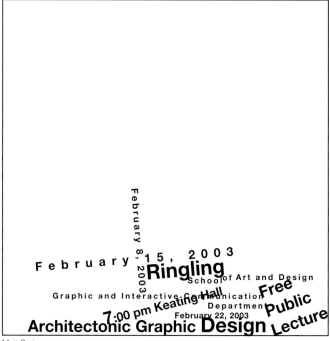

Matt Greiner

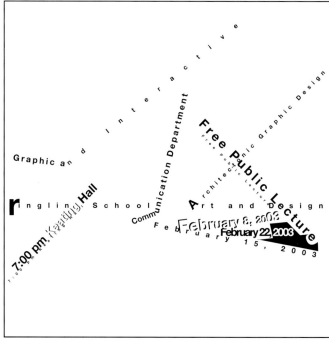

Matt Greiner

Lawrie Talansky

Study in one size, one weight for the composition to the right.

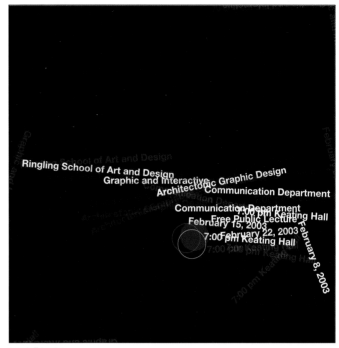

Lawrie Talansky

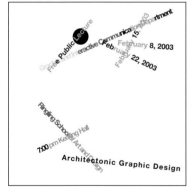

Giselle Guerrero

Study in one size, one weight for the composition to the right.

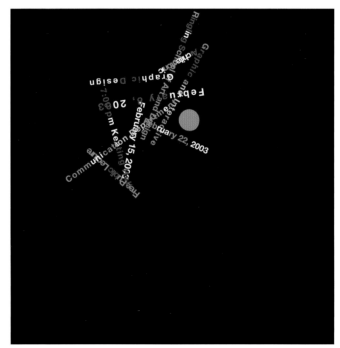

Giselle Guerrero

## Nonobjective Elements

The introduction of nonobjective elements can enhance random compositions through diversity of shape. These elements need to appear as unconstrained as the text in their form and placement. Occasionally, a nonobjective element can modify a word or line and improve communication in a chaotic environment.

The single black rule attached to the red circle in the composition below emphasizes the word "communication." It provides a starting point in reading, and its offset placement gives it a random feeling. The active works to the right show progression from a relatively legible version (top) to a much more active and fragmented work (bottom).

On the page opposite the smaller compositions are earlier one size, one weight thumbnail studies. Although the larger versions use a very similar type composition, they become more complex with the introduction of nonobjective elements. The irregularly shaped rules in the bottom composition particularly enhance the random visual language.

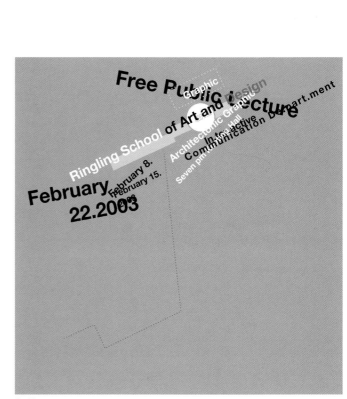

Jon Vautour

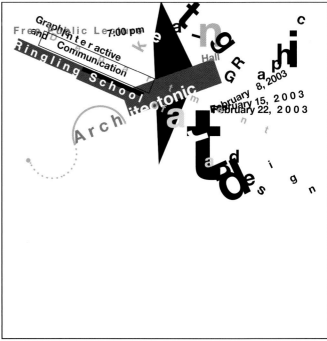

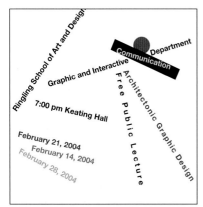

Melissa Pena

Jon Vautour

# Random System

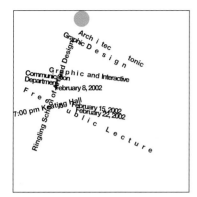

Katherine Chase

Study in one size, one weight for the nonobjective composition to the right.

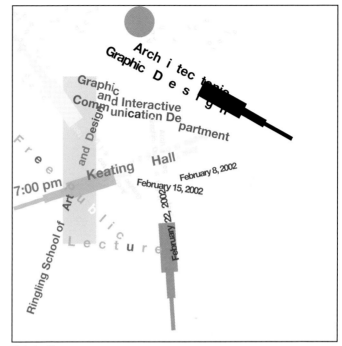

Katherine Chase

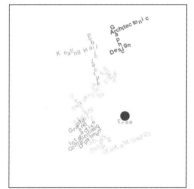

Chean Wei Law

Study in one size, one weight for the nonobjective composition to the right.

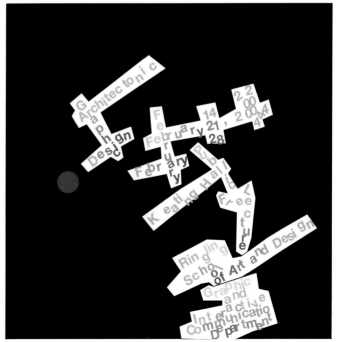

Chean Wei Law

## Shaped Background

The introduction of a shaped back-ground with unexpected angles increas-es the complexity of the composition. These backgrounds employ the same random angles as the type and become a counterpoint to the lines of text.

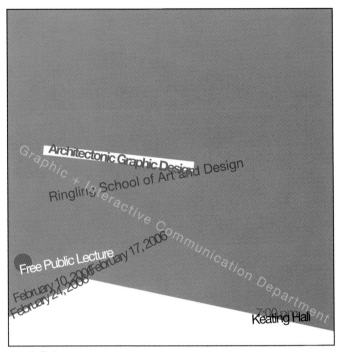

Amanda Clark

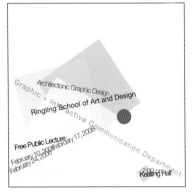

Amanda Clark

Early study for the composition to the right.

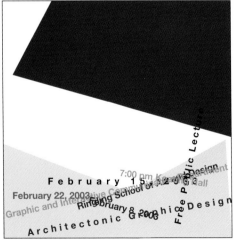

Jennifer Frykholm

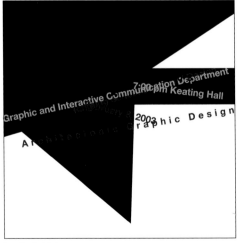

Jennifer Frykholm

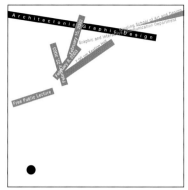

Loni Diep

Early study for the composition to the right.

Loni Diep

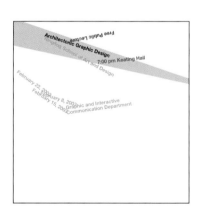

Casey Diehl

Early study for the composition to the right.

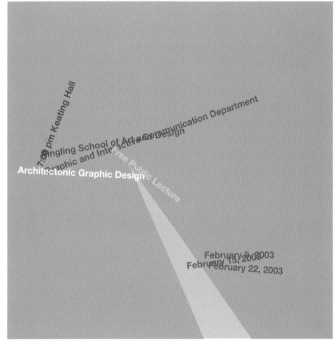

Casey Diehl

## Repetition

One of the traits of the random system is repetition, and excessive repetition of type elements in pursuit of an interesting textural composition rapidly leads to loss of communication. These works explore pattern and texture as compositional elements. While communication is subordinated to texture in the compositions on this page, the use of layering text on top of the texture, as seen in the composition opposite on the top, does preserve some communication. Another strategy that preserves communication, employed in the composition opposite on the bottom, is the enlarged repetition of the message, enhanced with color change and the use of uppercase text.

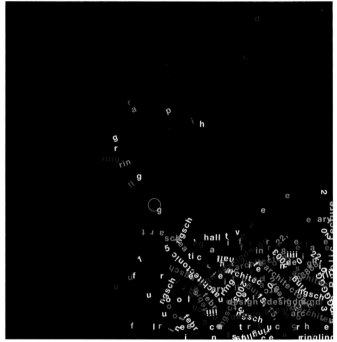

Pushpita Saha

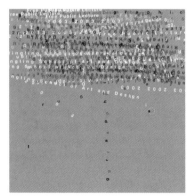

Pushpita Saha

Early study for the composition to the right.

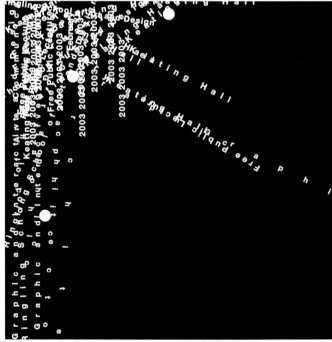

Pushpita Saha

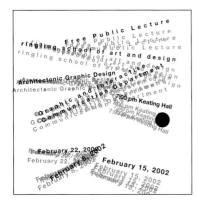

Chad Sawyer

Early study for the composition to the right.

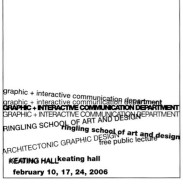

Wendy Gingerich

Early study for the composition to the right.

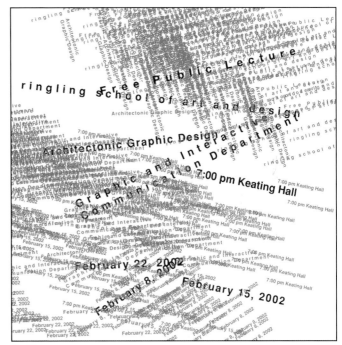

Chad Sawyer

Wendy Ellen Gingerich

5. Grid System

**Design with vertical and horizontal divisions**

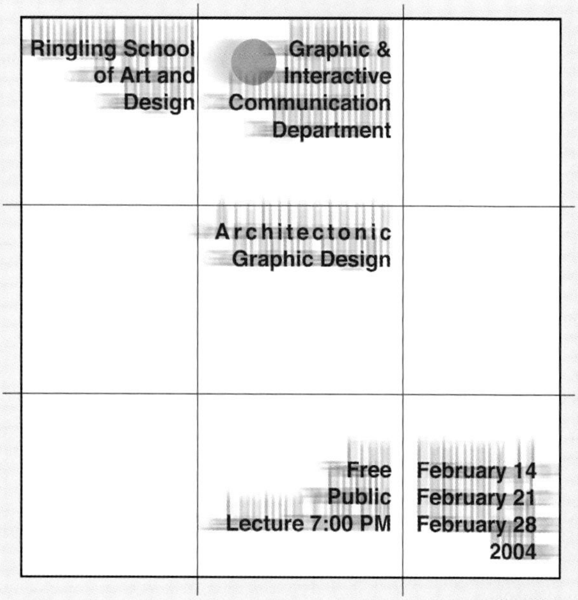

Ringling School
of Art and
Design

Graphic &
Interactive
Communication
Department

Architectonic
Graphic Design

Free
Public
Lecture 7:00 PM

February 14
February 21
February 28
2004

A grid is a system of vertical and horizontal divisions that organize and create relationships between elements. Grid system arrangements are usually formal and are intended to create visual order and economy in production. Examples of grid systems include windows, maps, and crossword puzzles. Grids are frequently used in publication design and web design as they guide information hierarchies and promote visual rhythm and consistency among multiple pages or screens.

The objective in organizing visual communication with the grid system is to develop strong interrelationships between the typographic elements and recurring rhythmical proportions of text blocks, images, and space. Grid systems differ from the axial system in that the visual relationships are not tied to a single axis and usually employ more than a single column.

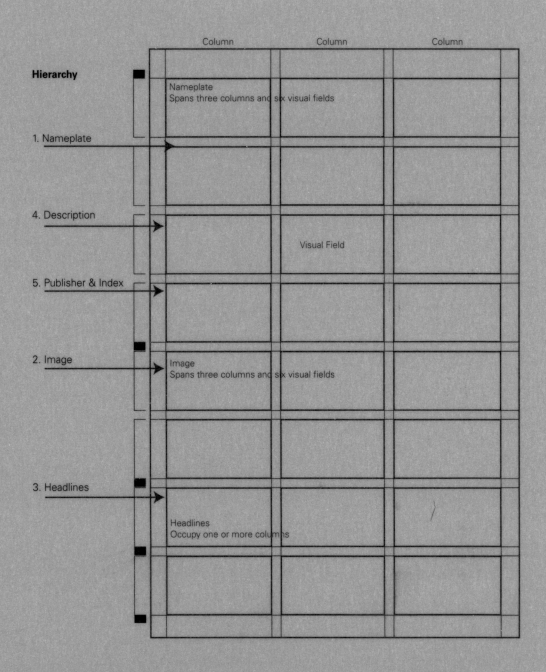

**Hierarchy**

1. Nameplate

4. Description

5. Publisher & Index

2. Image

3. Headlines

Column  Column  Column

Nameplate
Spans three columns and six visual fields

Visual Field

Image
Spans three columns and six visual fields

Headlines
Occupy one or more columns

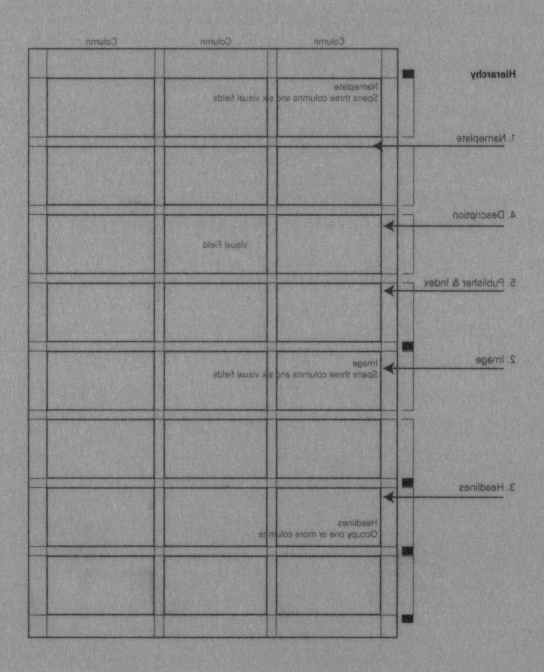

One of the hallmarks of the design work produced by Massimo Vignelli, Vignelli Associates, is a timeless classic approach to grid composition. The quintessential approach can be seen in the "Skyline, New York Architecture and Design Calendar." The "Skyline" grid is composed of three columns subdivided into eight visual fields. Images and text span columns and visual fields as needed, permitting flexibility and variety in the design of each issue. The system is orderly and the hierarchy is compelling as it invites the reader to readily engage the information.

The front page is divided into distinct areas through the use of heavy rules. The large bold title is emphasized by a rule above, separated from the publication and index by space and enclosed by another rule at mid-page. Additional rules separate the headlines.

Massimo Vignelli, 1978

The grid in the calendar program by Emil Ruder is determined by the strong vertical strokes of the large-scale letters representing the first character in the day of the week. The repetition of "mdmd" creates a rhythm in the right edge alignment of the columns and a tension with the closer column under the "f." Text in each column is grouped according to time. The strong stress of the vertical movement is in contrast to the negative counterforms of the letters.

The smaller work below, also by Ruder, uses a similar play of horizontal and vertical movement. The vertical stress is emphasized by the columns of text and intensified by the rules that separate lines of text. The horizontal movement is created by the sequence of bold arcs completing a circle.

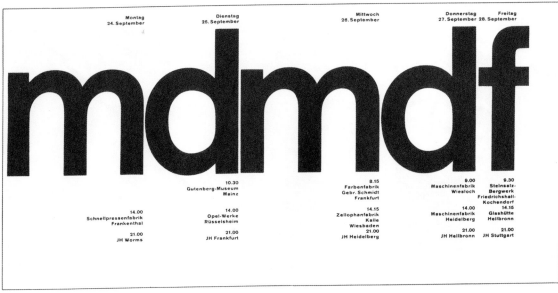

| Montag 24. September | Dienstag 25. September | Mittwoch 26. September | Donnerstag 27. September | Freitag 28. September |
|---|---|---|---|---|
| | 10.30 Gutenberg-Museum Mainz | 8.15 Farbenfabrik Gebr. Schmidt Frankfurt | 9.00 Maschinenfabrik Wiesloch | 9.30 Steinsalz-Bergwerk Friedrichshall-Kochendorf |
| 14.00 Schnellpressenfabrik Frankenthal | 14.00 Opel-Werke Rüsselsheim | 14.15 Zellophanfabrik Kalle Wiesbaden | 14.00 Maschinenfabrik Heidelberg | 14.15 Glashütte Heilbronn |
| 21.00 JH Worms | 21.00 JH Frankfurt | 21.00 JH Heidelberg | 21.00 JH Heilbronn | 21.00 JH Stuttgart |

Emil Ruder, c. 1960

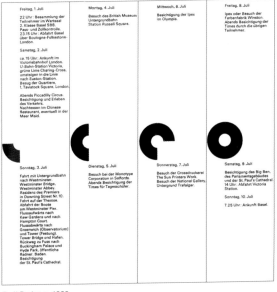

| Freitag, 1. Juli | Montag, 4. Juli | Mittwoch, 6. Juli | Freitag, 8. Juli |
|---|---|---|---|
| 22 Uhr: Besammlung der Teilnehmer im Wartsaal 2. Klasse Basel SBB. Pass- und Zollkontrolle. 23.15 Uhr: Abfahrt Basel über Boulogne-Folkestone-London. | Besuch des British Museum Untergrundbahn Station Russell Square. | Besichtigung der Ipex im Olympia. | Ipex oder Besuch der Farbenfabrik Winston. Abends Besichtigung der Times durch die übrigen Teilnehmer. |
| Samstag, 2. Juli | | | |
| ca. 15 Uhr: Ankunft im Victoriabahnhof London. U-Bahn-Station Victoria, grüne Linie Charing-Cross, umsteigen in die Linie nach Euston-Station. Bezug der Quartiere, 1. Taviatock Square, London. | | | |
| Abends Piccadilly Circus. Besichtigung und Erleben des Verkehrs. Nachtessen im Chinese Restaurant, eventuell in der Mear Maid. | | | |
| Sonntag, 3. Juli | Dienstag, 5. Juli | Donnerstag, 7. Juli | Samstag, 9. Juli |
| Fahrt mit Untergrundbahn nach Westminster. Westminster Bridge, Westminster Abbey. Residenz des Premiers in Downing Street Nr. 10. Fahrt auf der Themse. Abfahrt der Boote am Westminster Pier. Flussaufwärts nach Kew Gardens und nach Hampton Court. Flussabwärts nach Greenwich (Observatorium) und Tower (Festung). Tower Bridge und Hafen. Rückweg zu Fuss nach Buckingham Palace und Hyde Park, öffentliche Radner. Baden. Besichtigung der St. Paul's Cathedral. | Besuch bei der Monotype Corporation in Salfords. Abends Besichtigung der Times für Tagesschüler. | Besuch der Grossdruckerei The Sun Printers Work. Besuch der National Gallery. Untergrund Trafalgar. | Besichtigung des Big Ben, des Parlamentsgebäudes und der St. Paul's Cathedral. 14 Uhr: Abfahrt Victoria Station. |
| | | | Sonntag, 10. Juli |
| | | | 7.25 Uhr: Ankunft Basel. |

Emil Ruder, c. 1960

# Grid System

Design for the screen poses unique challenges for grid design. Grid frameworks need to be flexible because information is variable and subject to viewer selection. Issues of navigation and changes in the volume of text make design problematic. The Vibrato web site uses a five-column grid and organizes the text with both columns and fields of color. The name, Vibrato, and the index on a yellow field are constants in design. Heads and important text appear in red as needed, and a light blue field highlights subordinate columns of text.

**VIBRATO** Naming, Inc.

| | | Solutions | | |
|---|---|---|---|---|
| Who we are<br>How we create vibrant names<br>Why vibrant?<br>Solutions<br>Collaborations<br>Clients speak<br>Process<br>Meet Vibrato<br>Position papers<br>Contact | | Re-Naming<br>Launches<br>Retail<br>Products<br>Film Titles<br>Taglines<br>Nomenclature | | |
| | As You Like It | Berried Treasures | Dex<br>Challenge: The New Yellow Pages<br>Positioning: Easy access to information you need | Go Figure |
| | LEGENDairy | Nectar Imperial | | *Strategy by Diefenbach Elkins |

---

**VIBRATO** Naming, Inc.

Who we are
How we create vibrant names
Why vibrant?
Solutions
Collaborations
Clients speak
Process
Meet Vibrato
Position papers
Contact

Our process empowers us to deliver vibrant solutions.

**Process**

1. Situation, Intent, and Opportunity Study
2. Name Creation: NomenCulture™
3. Report Development
4. Client Decision

First Wave Name Generation
- For each facet of each naming path, explore literal and symbolic lexicons
- Harvest a new lexicon: words and morphemes
- Cross-pollinate words, morphemes and ideas
- Self-refine and recommend naming candidates with rationale using client's strategic objectives and Vibrato's creative standards
- Collate into a first wave master list

Review/Refinements and Second Wave by Senior Team
- Review and score first wave master list
- Explore literal and symbolic lexicons with tighter focus
- Cross-pollinate and self-refine
- Recommend naming candidates with rationale
- Submit and collate with first wave master list into a final master list

---

**VIBRATO** Naming, Inc.

Who we are
How we create vibrant names
Why vibrant?
Solutions
Collaborations
Clients speak
Process
Meet Vibrato
Position papers
Contact

When your brand can inspire and persuade the people who are vital to your success, you can compete.

We help companies become more valuable by creating vibrant brand names for global businesses, products, and services. Names that both resound above the marketplace uproar and resonate with the constituencies among your audience—from your target market, current employees, potential recruits, industry press, to your prospective investors and merger partners.

---

**VIBRATO** Naming, Inc.

Who we are
How we create vibrant names
Why vibrant?
Solutions
Collaborations
Clients speak
Process
Meet Vibrato
Position papers
Contact

**Clients Speak**

BrandNew Consulting
Frontera Corporation
Hilton & DoubleTree Hotels
H.P. Hood
Jettis
Lexis-Nexis
Protocol
siegelgale
Soulells Studio
St. Aubyn
Wechsler Ross & Partners

"The thoroughness of her process, along with her creative energy, led to a winning product name every time. Meredith brings skill and artistry to every project."
Tisha Gray, Marketing Director
Lexis-Nexis

---

**VIBRATO** Naming, Inc.

Who we are
How we create vibrant names
Why vibrant?
Solutions
Collaborations
Clients speak
Process
Meet Vibrato
Position papers
Contact

Because mindshare drives marketshare

**Why Vibrant?**

A vibrant brand name **resounds** to:
- Assert your differential advantage
- Capture attention
- Rankle your competition
- Begin building recognition
- Be unquestionably memorable

And **resonates** to:
- Shoulder as much of your marketing burden as possible
- Initiate a meaningful, relevant, and persuasive relationship with your audience
- Reflect the voice, spirit, and values of your offering
- Set appropriate expectations, allowing for the evolution of your offering, technology, and social mores
- Be worth remembering

Intersection Studio

91

The grid system gives the designer an opportunity to explore horizontal composition in more familiar and orderly ways. Experience with the other systems has made the designer comfortable with changing texture through spacing, changing grouping through line breaks, and in consciously creating interesting white space.

Similar to the axial system, the grid system depends on alignment but differs in that there is more than a single axis. Using two or more columns increases the number of choices for alignment and interrelationship. The shapes of the textures and white spaces are rectangular, and the proportion of the spaces are important in composition.

### Initial Phase

Designers beginning work with the grid system recall skills gained during successful experiences with the axial system. Even early compositions are achieved with fluidity due to past experience. Two-column compositions are the most common during this phase.

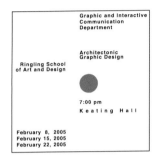

### Intermediate Phase

Experiments with tight and loose tracking create variations in texture that differentiate groups of text. Lines are broken at will to create narrow columns and strong alignments between groups of text.

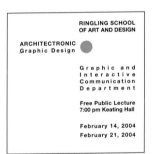

### Advanced Phase

Investigations focus on consciously creating interesting compositional space. An appreciation of the drama of large volumes of white negative space is developed and rhythms with the three repetitive dates are created.

## Grid System, Thumbnail Variations

Curiously, student work with grid composition in the context of the eight systems is different than the first work in development of grid compositions (see *Grid Systems*, K. Elam, Princeton Architectural Press). The compositions are more inventive and less predictable. There seems to be a deeper level of understanding typographic nuance and a more fluid execution gained with experience in the range of other systems.

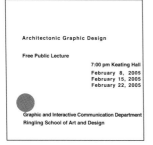

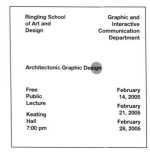

## Groups and Subgroups

Tracking the text creates changes in texture and tone. In the composition to the right subgroups are created within the title, "architectonic graphic design." All three words read as a single group in a tight justified rectangle, and "graphic design" is set off by the wider tracking. Tightly tracked text creates the darkest gray, normal tracking a mid gray, and wide tracking a light gray. The mix of changes in tone enhances the composition by providing change and variety. The group and subgroup strategy is employed continuously throughout this work and in similar compositions.

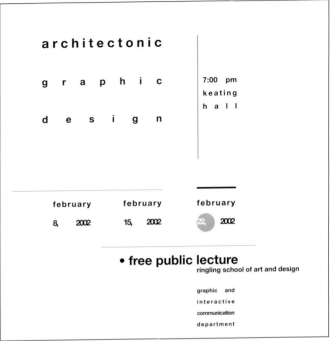

Bruce Kirkpatrick

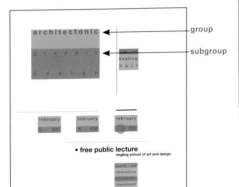

Bruce Kirkpatrick

## Tone

All of these compositions use tone to create and control the hierarchy. The selective use of black text in the work to the right guides the viewer to the time, place, and dates. The designer is also aware of the negative spaces that are created by the text alignments. Three large open rectangles of negative space provide a visual rest and counterpoint to the occupied rectangles.

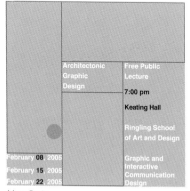

Mona Bagla

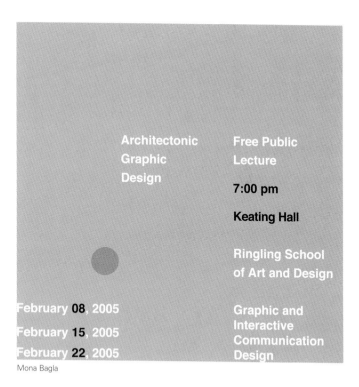

Mona Bagla

Laura Kate Jenkins

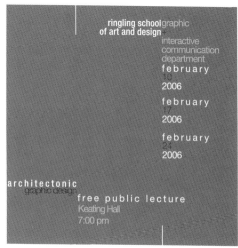

Phillip Clark

## Tone

Although the grid structures in these works are simple and use only minimal nonobjective elements, the eye flow is changed in subtle ways. The text is grouped to simplify the compositions and the groups are accented with changes in color or tone. Position of the groups, tone, and negative space amplifies the hierarchy.

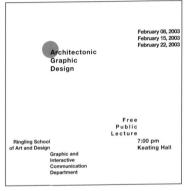

Dustin Blouse

Study in one size, one weight for the nonobjective composition to the right.

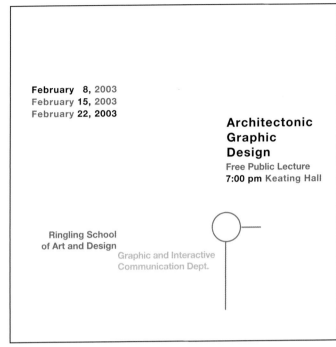

Dustin Blouse

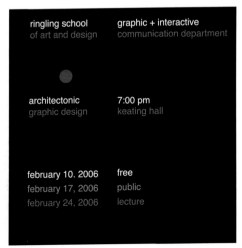

Trish Tatman

Lara Carvalho

# Grid System

## Rhythm and Direction

The gray pattern of rules in this work has a dual purpose. The rules define the two left columns, and their rhythm and movement gently guides the eye to the center of the format. The definition of space is crisp and the negative shapes are a series of rectangles. A similar strategy is used below to introduce rhythm and to emphasize the title.

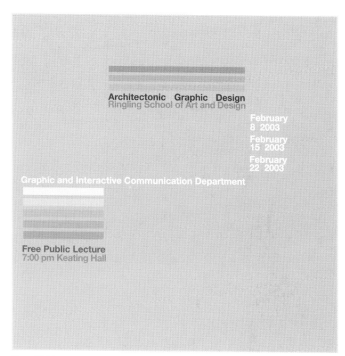

Casey Diehl

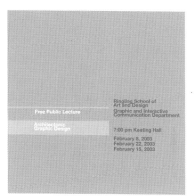

Casey Diehl

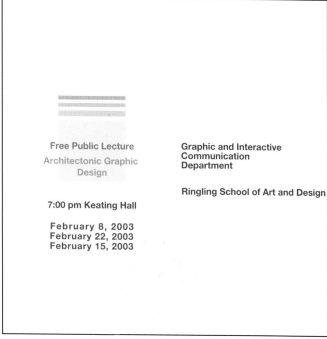

Casey Diehl

## Shaped Format

The black perimeter format line is purposely left out of the work to the right so that the white background invades the compositional space and becomes part of the work. The bottom right corner contains only a hint of the format corner. The idea that the text and limited nonobjective elements float in space is intriguing. A similar idea is used below whereby the circle is cropped out of the corner of the format.

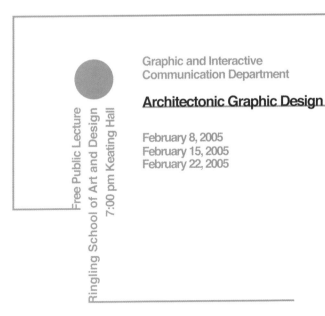

Christian Andersen

Eva Bodok

Study in one size, one weight for the nonobjective composition to the right.

Eva Bodok

**Horizontal Vertical**

The combination of horizontal and vertical text makes these compositions engaging. In the composition to the right the lines are used as structural elements to convey information and create movement. The single long horizontal line of text acts to separate groups of text and is accented with red dates. Separating of the text into two groups as in the example below yields a simple and effective grid structure.

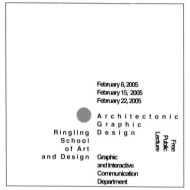

Elizabeth Centolella

Study in one size, one weight for the nonobjective composition to the right.

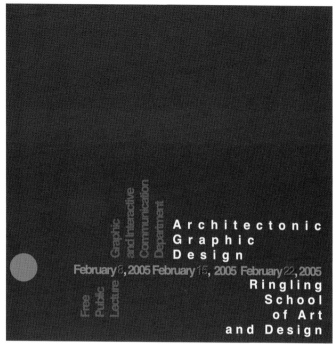

Elizabeth Centolella

Study in one size, one weight for the nonobjective composition to the right.

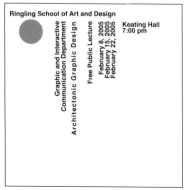

Christian Andersen

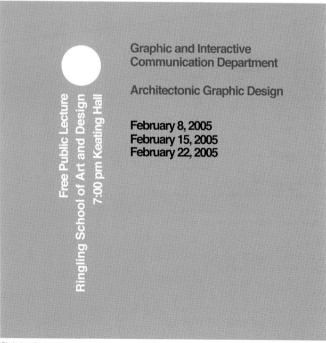

Christian Andersen

## Nonobjective Structure

In these works the nonobjective elements take the form of a strong structure to complement the composition. The format on the right is complex; it is divided into three columns and twelve visual fields. This structure is greatly simplified by highlighting only the horizontal visual fields. Horizontal movement is intensified by long lines of text that span columns, the white rectangular shape at top, and the two white rules. The alignment of text (flush left), contrasts with the horizontal flow, and the eye is pulled both down and across the composition. Similarly, the work below uses strong horizontal fields to group the text, and the vertical movement is implied by the flush left alignment in each column.

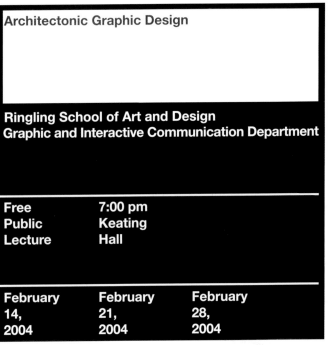

Mike Plymale

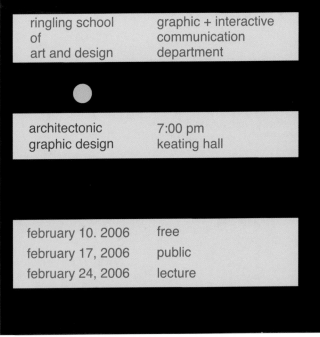

Trish Tatman

## Nonobjective Structure

This series looks at both strong vertical and horizontal movement through non-objective structure. The placement of the type is essentially the same in both large examples, but the composition changes dramatically depending on the direction of the rules. In the example to the right, vertical rules that align with the top of the text emphasize the columns. Below right, horizontal rules that separate each of the three groups emphasize the visual fields. The title is changed from two lines to a single line to enhance the horizontal flow.

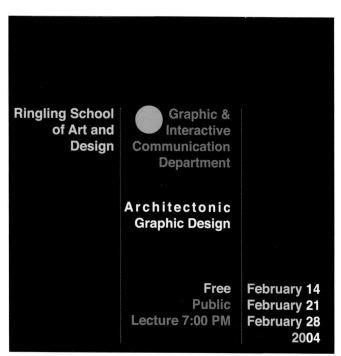

Sarah Al-wassia

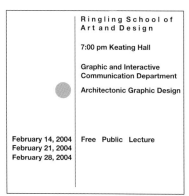

Sarah Al-wassia

Study in one size, one weight for the non-objective composition to the right.

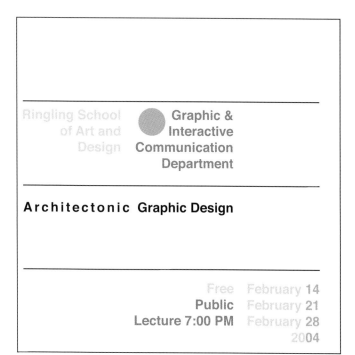

Sarah Al-wassia

## Transparent Structure

Transparent structures identify the columns and visual fields that make up a grid. In the works to the right and bottom right, each column is a gray field. These gray fields are accented by transparent horizontal fields that overlap the columns to separate type into visual fields or provide emphasis. The result is a visible structure that divides the space. The work below left uses a different strategy to create transparency. The red outline square emphasizes the word "Architectonic" and becomes a transparent window.

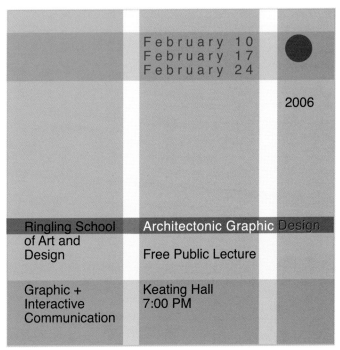

Alex Evans

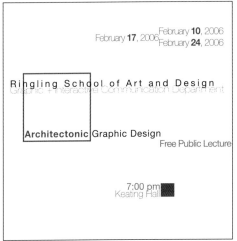

Amanda Clark

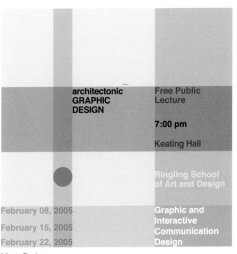

Mona Bagla

## Transparent Structure

The delicacy and visual interest created by overlapping transparent gray tones is highlighted in this work. Each group of text occupies a rectangle created by gray tones emphasizing an architectonic structure. The tonal changes are accompanied by an equally delicate type treatment of small-scale lightweight text.

The structure of the composition below is also revealed by transparency. The left and right columns that hold text are vertical transparent planes. Visual fields are shown in a similar manner with horizontal planes. Visual interest is created where horizontal planes and a vertical plane overlap the circle.

Loni Diep

Loni Diep

Study in one size, one weight for the non-objective composition to the right.

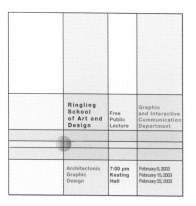

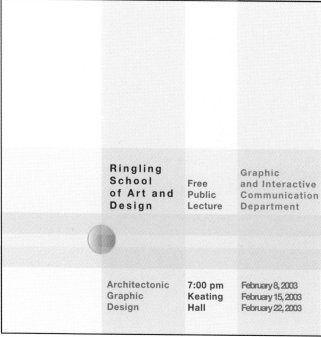

Laura Kate Jenkins

6. Transitional System

**Design with shifted bands and layers**

RINGLING SCHOOL OF ART AND DESIGN
Graphic and Interactive
Communication Department
Architectonic
Graphic Design

Free Public Lecture
7:00 pm Keating Hall

February 14, 2004
February 21, 2004
February 28, 2004

The transitional system of visual organization is an informal system of layered and shifted banding. There are not inter-relationships along an axis or edge alignments, and elements move freely left and right. This is a far more casual system than the grid system in that strict interrelationship through edge alignment is not desirable. The lines of type are free-flowing and the textures they create assist in ordering the message. Examples of natural transitional arrangements include strata of layered rock or casually stacked wood.

Compositions can be airy and widely leaded or tightly com-pact, which emphasizes the negative space. This system often results in compositions that echo fine art in that many have the visual feel of a landscape, which is admittedly enhanced by the use of the circle element that becomes an abstract sun or moon.

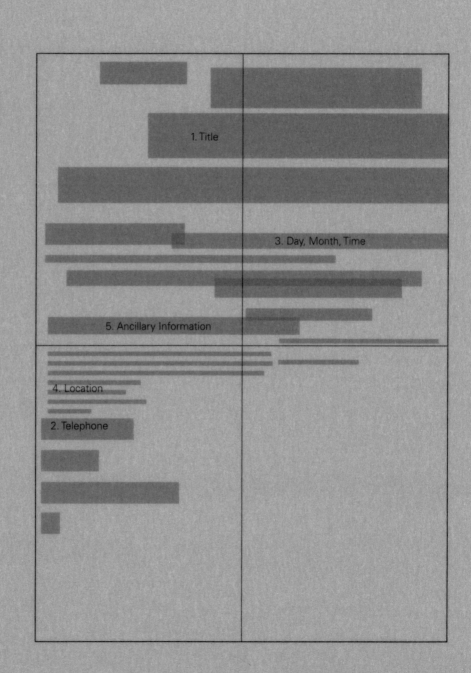

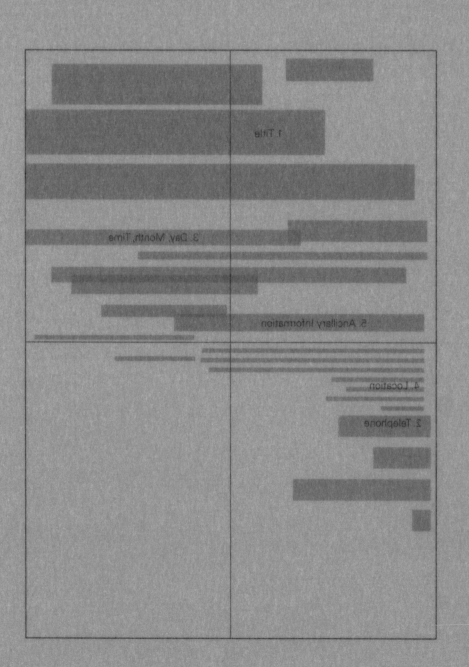

David Carson has never been bound by tradition or the way things are typically done. He challenges the viewer to be as involved with the aesthetics of the message as the message itself. His distinctive visual language frequently involves a transitional system that is characterized by fluid composition and the layering of type. However, within this casual style there is order. In the End of Print poster the text is grouped by size, color, and font. The title advances toward the viewer in large green text. The day, month, and time of the presentation are mostly in outline type punctuated by a green-filled date and time. Additional information is in small-scale text that is regularly spaced for the more important information and widely spaced for the less important details. The result is a carefully controlled transitional collage of texture and space.

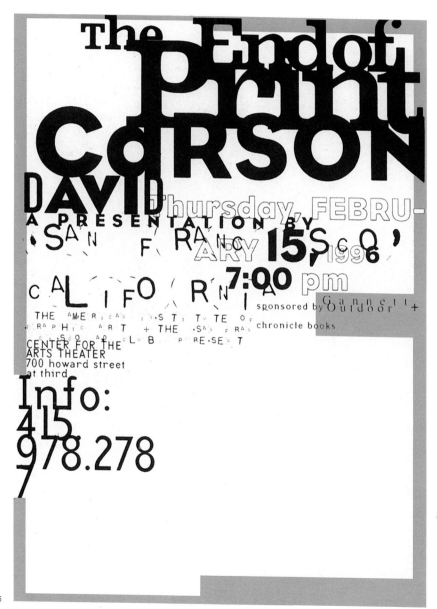

David Carson, 1996

## Transitional System

The works on this spread are free-form works that David Carson created for the Swiss newspaper *Die Welwoche* for the issue published on the opening day of his exhibition in Bern. The posters are a collage of fonts and textures that lead the eye across, through, and down the page. Italic text emphasizes the horizontal transitional movement, and rests are created for the eye with roman text and the dot of the exclamation point.

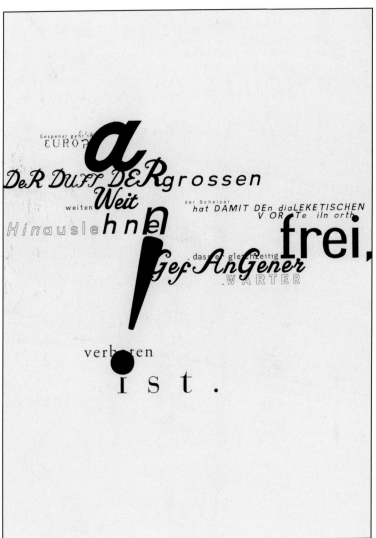

David Carson, 1997

David Carson, 1997

The transitional system is the most informal and relaxed system because the elements are not required to align on any axis. Indeed, unaligned elements are encouraged, and fluid movement is one of the strongest traits of the system. The most difficult aspect of the system for most designers is overcoming the need to interrelate elements through alignment. Instead, elements are related through the massing of texture and the shapes of those textures on the page.

The beauty of the transitional system is in its natural asymmetry. The lines of text float through the format, creating textures and white space. Grouping lines to create denser

### Initial Phase

Initial work explores the designer's adjustment to the freedom of free line placement.

### Intermediate Phase

Informal grouping is carefully considered as is the movement of lines of text down the page. Lines and groups are differentiated through tracking with contrast between denser darker and wider lighter textures.

### Advanced Phase

As work progresses the sensitivity to texture and white space plays an important role. The overwhelming proportion of white space to textured space becomes startling and interesting.

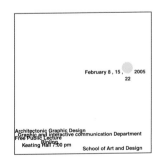

darker textures or lighter more airy textures remains an important concern. Massed lines of text can be separated and differentiated by tracking to create additional changes in texture. While readability is diminished, careful control of the text tone and placement can create a message that communicates.

## Movement

One of the strongest traits of the transitional system is a sense of movement. Since there are no strong vertical alignments to create a visual stop, the typography seems to be in motion, a sense that is intensified when rules or text bleed off of the left or right edges of the format.

Experience with grouping gained by working with other systems is brought to the transitional system and logical groups of lines share proximity relationships. Sensitivity to the message leads the designer to create a natural reading order and differentiate the groups by positioning or a change in tone.

In the composition to the right, the thin line entering the format and attached to the tiny circle emphasizes movement. The text above and below the rule continues the movement toward the right edge. Below, staggered multiple lines enhance the feeling of motion as they move toward and away from the text groups.

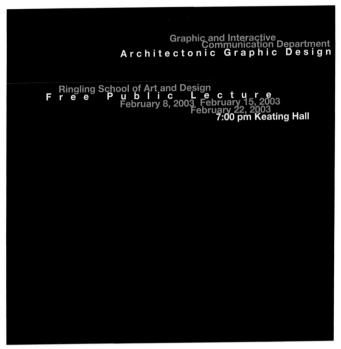

Lawrie Talansky

Lawrie Talansky

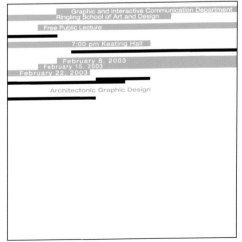

Loni Diep

## Movement

Nonobjective elements can complement the typography in creating a sense of movement. The wedge shapes in the compositions to the right and below right introduce a diagonal along which type slides. The motion (below left) is more a sense of vibration as the text is repeated in the background, creating a gray textured background for the message in black.

Pushpita Saha

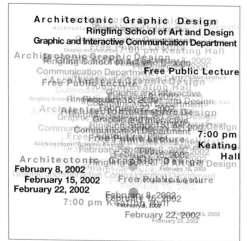

Mei Suwaid

Rebekah Wilkins

## Change in Direction

Designers experimenting with the transitional system often develop unexpected relationships. These works employ the anticipated horizontal movement but also contrast it with a vertical direction. The contrast is striking in the composition to the right as the eye comes to a screeching halt where horizontal and vertical type meet.

The works below use the contrast in direction in a less forceful manner. The early study separates the type into two relatively equal groups in opposite directions, but the contrast feels unresolved. The later work uses only one line of text on the vertical, for both counterpoint and emphasis.

Anthony Orsa

Jeff Bucholtz

Study in one size, one weight for the non-objective composition to the right.

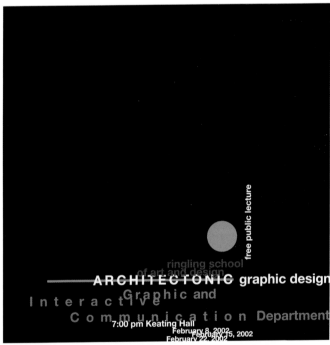

Jeff Bucholtz

## Change in Direction

These compositions contrast in both direction and texture. Masses of text are contrasted with a single line. In the composition to the right the large negative space surrounds the title and gives the one horizontal line considerable emphasis. A similar play in negative space is used in both works below. The vertical text is loosely tracked to add further contrast to the denser texture and change in direction.

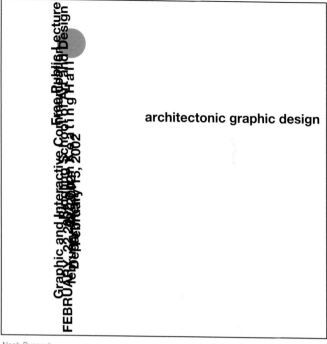

Noah Rusnock

Pushpita Saha

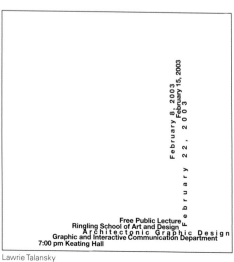

Lawrie Talansky

## Nonobjective Elements

The dramatic use of nonobjective elements makes transitional compositions lively and complex. Nonobjective planes and rules can hold text or provide a background texture.

In the composition to the right, transparent planes are attached to each line of type and move into the format from the top as they shift and overlap. Below left a black rule emphasizes the department name, and repeated rules become a background for the type. Multiple overlapping rules below right move through the format to become a textured background for the type.

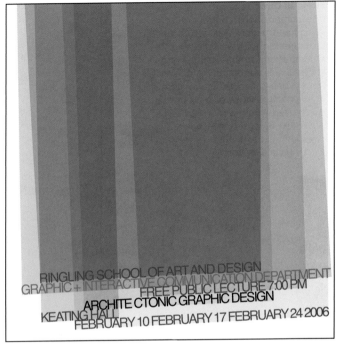

Alex Evans

Michael Johnston

Willie Diaz

## Nonobjective Elements

This series of compositions works with multiple rules that act as grounds to emphasize lines of text. The circle becomes an element that ties the composition together by overlapping and attaching to the two rule groups. Even without the type the composition is satisfying.

Phillip Clark

Study of nonobjective elements for the composition to the right.

Phillip Clark

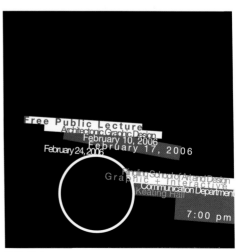

Phillip Clark

## Diagonal Direction

Because the transitional system is closely tied to the idea of movement, the diagonal direction is a natural extension. The diagonal is the most dynamic direction and the sense of movement is enhanced. Fluid simplicity and the restrained use of changes in tone make the diagonal composition to the right enticing. The white circle provides a starting point, and change in tone emphasizes two important lines of text and creates a hierarchy. Below, movement is accentuated by the use of rules that bleed off of the page. All of the type seems to be in motion because of the staggering of words in tightly related groups.

Casey Diehl

Jorge Lamora

**Visual Language**
The rules and traits of the transitional system are refined into a visual language by this designer. Four works all by the same designer enjoy a generous volume of white negative space. The negative space becomes a part of a visual language where there is a strong sense of movement in the compositions. Lines of text are welded to the composition as they touch fields of tone and merge.

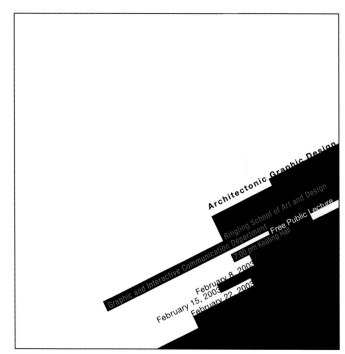

Loni Diep

Studies in one size, one weight for the non-objective compositions.

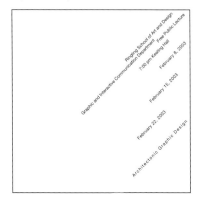

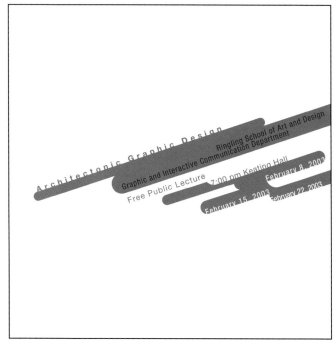

Loni Diep

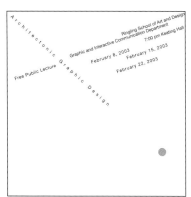

Loni Diep

Loni Diep

**Design with standardized units**

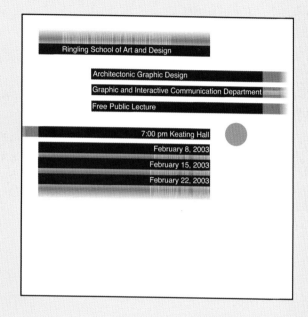

The modular system is dependent on standardized non-objective elements or units that act as a ground to hold and contain text. Compositions are created by the organization and placement of the modular units. Examples of the modular system include building blocks, storage containers, and component systems.

Typographic lines and words have a distinctly individual form that defy standardization and require a module that acts as a ground. Modules can be as simple as a hairline square or rectangle or more complex geometric shapes such as circles, ellipses, triangles, etc.

The idea is to standardize the unit on which the typography rests and then compose the message with the modules. Lines of type can be broken or split into multiple lines at will, which, like grouping, assists in communicating the message.

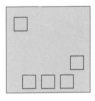

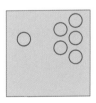

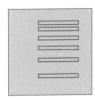

## Modular System

The smallest module possible is one that holds only one character. Philippe Apeloig's poster for a French language event isolates each character to emphasize the characteristics of language. The individual modules are accentuated by a colored background in a checkerboard pattern. This makes the composition complex and highly active, and the viewer has to focus carefully in order to be able to read.

The slash, also called the solidus, is a symbol used for phonemic transcription of speech. Here, it becomes an appropriate element to fill the empty modules that surround the words and provides visual punctuation with meaning.

Philippe Apeloig, 2004

The modules for Philippe Apeloig's Bresil (Brazil) poster fluctuate in size as they move through the page. The colors, reminiscent of Latin American culture, alternate from module to module. Shapes are created by individual letterforms, repeated letterforms, rectangles with reversed out letterforms, and by the background that enters counterform spaces. Shifting modules and changing scale brings variety to the work.

Philippe Apeloig, 2005

Heebok Lee, Dan Boyarski

A square framework organizes complex information for a presentation about Designing with Time. Each module contains text or image clues to the content and links to further information. Modules are identified with gray grid rules, and the information is cropped so as to be both informative and enticing.

## Modular System

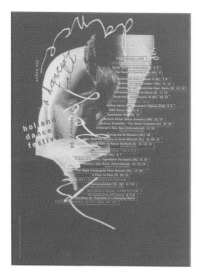

In Bob van Dijk's poster rectangular modules contrast with a highly abstract photograph and irregular lines. Intriguingly, the modules are enclosed on the right side, creating a solid rhythm of repeated rectangles, and open on the left side as they move toward the image. The modules bring order to the complex composition and clarity to the list of twenty-two different dance venues.

Design: Studio Dumbar (Bob van Dijk), 1998
Photography: Deen van Meer

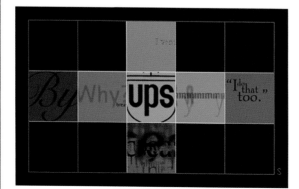

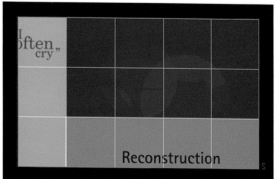

## Modular System, Thumbnail Variations

The thumbnail phase of the modular system is unlike the other systems; it involves nonobjective elements in all compositions, even the one size, one weight thumbnails. Modules take the place of nonobjective elements, and the designer is challenged to design with modular shapes at the outset. Simple shapes such as circle, square, and rectangle are the easiest to control, with long rectangles having the closest visual relationship to lines of text. Polygons, ellipses, and other multifaceted shapes become very complex and are much more difficult to control.

Early compositions often contain stand-alone modules, but as work progresses modules begin to touch, overlap, and combine so as to create other interesting shapes. In working

### Initial Phase
During the initial phase modules are rigid and awkward in the format, and designers discover how difficult it is to work with complex shapes.

### Intermediate Phase
Simple regular shapes that more comfortably hold text replace more complex shapes. Designers explore regularity, with an emphasis on communication.

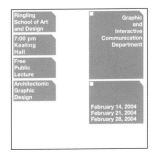

### Advanced Phase
Designers experiment with overlapping modules and more casual text placement. Attention is given to composition, overlapping modules, and negative space.

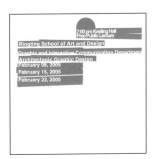

through the thumbnail process the designer realizes that the lines of text can be arranged in the shapes in an irregular manner and that the modules need not be regimented, which results in more lively compositions.

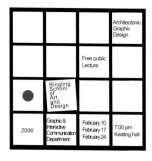

## Circle Modules

Circles are problematic modular elements; the circle is the most visually compelling geometric form and a circle silently screams for attention even when used in a small scale. In addition, the circle has no corners or edges for alignment or creating interrelationships with other elements.

The examples on this page use informal composition and employ overlapping to achieve unity. The use of the semicircle as a sub-module and the cropped and irregularly oriented text groups brings diversity to the composition. The outline red circles accent the composition, and by overlapping, facilitate cohesiveness—when elements touch or overlap they feel as if they belong to each other. A similar strategy is used below left as the outline red circle overlaps the two gray circles to create a relationship and unify the composition. Transparency and overlapping perform a similar unifying function in the composition below right.

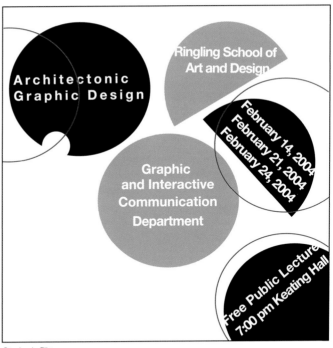

Stephanie Flis

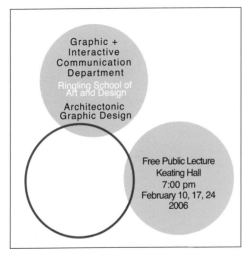

Michael Johnston

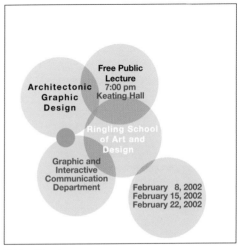

Keishea Edwards

## Circle Modules

These examples use regimented compositions unified through regularity and visual interest created by diversity within that regularity. The work to the right is strongly regimented, but the missing circle and the red accent circle bring interest to the composition. Although the red circle below is offset for emphasis, the placement of the circle modules is patterned. The designer brings variety to the composition by cropping the circles from the right edge and rotating the type for a more comfortable fit.

Michael Johnston

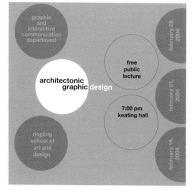

Elsa Chaves

Early study for the composition to the right.

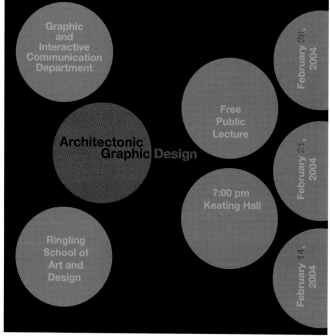

Elsa Chaves

## Square Modules

The square modules in these examples have a strong relationship to the grid system. Grids are composed of both columns and visual fields; the modules can be regarded as square visual fields. In this case what makes the modular system interesting is that the designer composes with the square modules much more freely. The modules can differ in tone or shift and rotate. Type can align within the module or attach to an edge, as well as change tone.

The examples on this page use a regular grid. Selectively eliminating modules brings variety and interest to the grid and highlights the three outlined date modules. Variation also occurs through the change in tone and red accents, which also create hierarchal order.

Mike Plymale

Mike Plymale

Mike Plymale

## Square Modules

The eye loves diversity within unity, and an irregularly placed square module provides that diversity in these works. The offset module in the composition to the right contrasts with the regularity of the other modules. Type placed along the very edge of the module allows the background white to invade each black square in an irregular fashion. The highly capricious compositions below take a more informal approach in that the type is only loosely grouped on the modules. Words are broken at will and overlap the bounds of the modules.

Andrea Cannistra

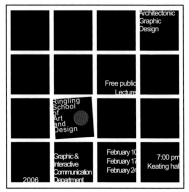

Azure Harper

Eva Bodok

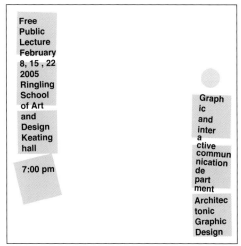

Eva Bodok

## Rectangle Modules

Long rectangles readily correspond to the shape of lines of text and feel comfortable as modules for type. Composition is satisfying as well in that the lines can be logically arranged and evenly spaced. Variation occurs as the lines of text vary in length, texture, and tone. The circle and the red accent guide the hierarchy and provide an unexpected counterpoint to the strongly regular compositions.

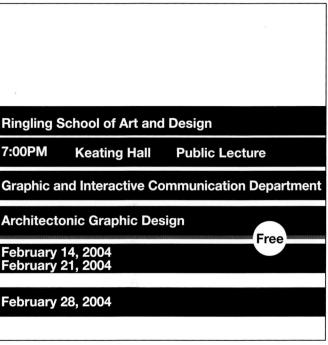

Chean Wei Law

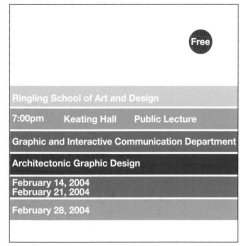

Chean Wei Law

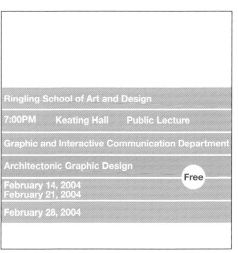

Chean Wei Law

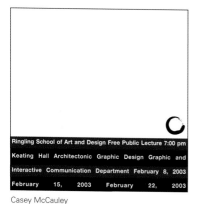

Ringling School of Art and Design Free Public Lecture 7:00 pm Keating Hall Architectonic Graphic Design Graphic and Interactive Communication Department February 8, 2003 February 15, 2003 February 22, 2003

Casey McCauley

Ringling School of Art and Design

Architectonic Graphic Design

Graphic and Interactive Communication Department

Free Public Lecture

7:00 pm Keating Hall

February 8, 2003

February 15, 2003

February 22, 2003

Casey McCauley

Graphic + Interactive Communication Department

7:00 pm Free Public Lecture Keating Hall

Architectonic Graphic Design

Ringling School of Art and Design

February 10, 2006  February 24, 2006

February 17, 2006

Amanda Clark

ARCHITECTONIC GRAPHIC DESIGN

Graphic + Interactive Communication Department

Ringling School of Art and Design

Free Public Lecture

7:00 pm Keating Hall

February 10, 17, 24, 2006

Willie Diaz

### Rectangle Modules

Variations can occur in a composition of rectangles when the modules are released from regimentation. Once modules are free to move in space they can change angle, shift and be cropped off of an edge, and overlap to become new shapes. Compositions are energized by the change in space and the change to irregular shapes. The background space is distinctly uneven in these works. Areas where modules overlap become points of compositional interest.

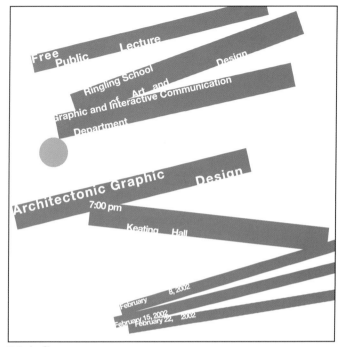

Katherine Chase

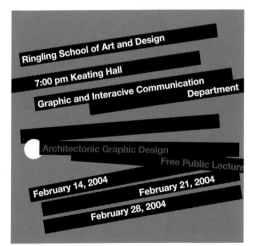

Sara Suter

Sara Suter

Christian Andersen

Early study for the composition to the right.

Christian Andersen

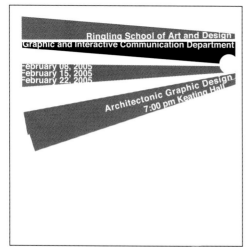

Christian Andersen

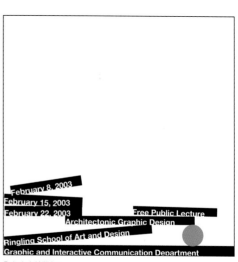

Rebekah Wilkins

## Transparency

Compositions become more complex when rectangular modules are both free-floating in space and transparent. Negative background space is divided irregularly, and the positive space of the rectangles creates new shapes as they overlap. Lighter and denser textures play on each other as rectangles move in front or behind.

Elizabeth Centolella

Elizabeth Centolella

Chloe Price

### Transparency

Outlined rectangles communicate a similar sense of transparency and are still more complex, since the eye is engaged with the strokes of the letter forms and the outline shapes of the rectangles. The change in space is engaging and the line repetition is energizing. Rectangles can overlap, as they do in the composition below right, to highlight and emphasize important words.

Jonathon Seniw

Jonathon Seniw

Heidi Dyer

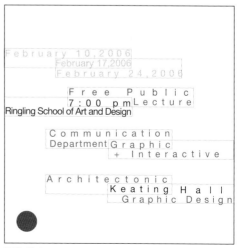

Phillip Clark

## 8. Bilateral System

**Design that is symmetrical to an axis**

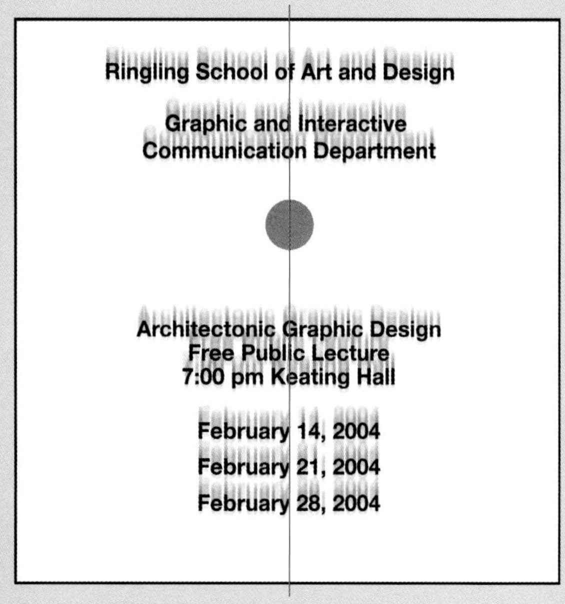

Ringling School of Art and Design

Graphic and Interactive
Communication Department

Architectonic Graphic Design
Free Public Lecture
7:00 pm Keating Hall

February 14, 2004
February 21, 2004
February 28, 2004

The bilateral system is the most symmetrical of the visual organization systems. It consists of a single axis with lines of text centered on the axis. Examples of the bilateral system include the human body, butterflies, leaves, and many animals and man-made objects.

As the most symmetrical system, the bilateral system is the most challenging compositionally. This is due to the inherent symmetry that makes these compositions predictable and potentially uninteresting. Placing the axis off center in the format can immediately make the composition more dynamic. A diagonal axis can bring a bit more visual interest to the composition, as does moving a line of text diagonally off of the baseline. The addition of nonobjective elements to the composition can transform the work to one of heightened visual interest.

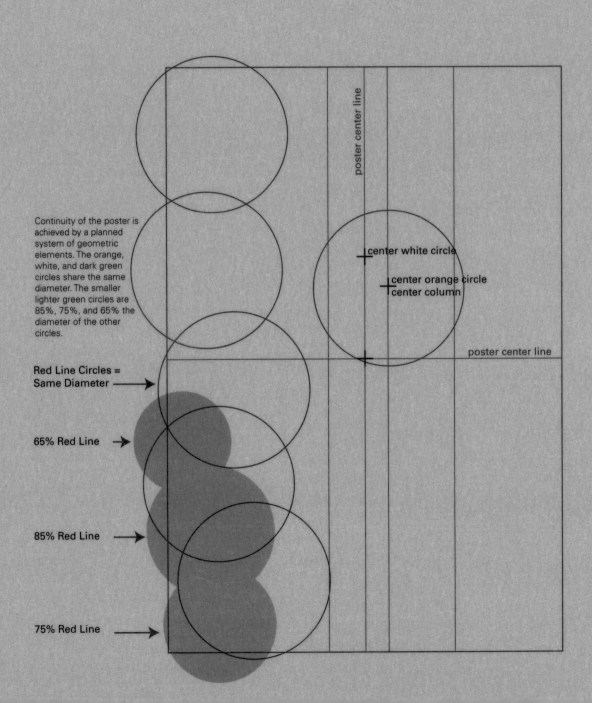

poster center line

Continuity of the poster is achieved by a planned system of geometric elements. The orange, white, and dark green circles share the same diameter. The smaller lighter green circles are 85%, 75%, and 65% the diameter of the other circles.

center white circle

center orange circle
center column

poster center line

Red Line Circles = Same Diameter ➔

65% Red Line ➔

85% Red Line ➔

75% Red Line ➔

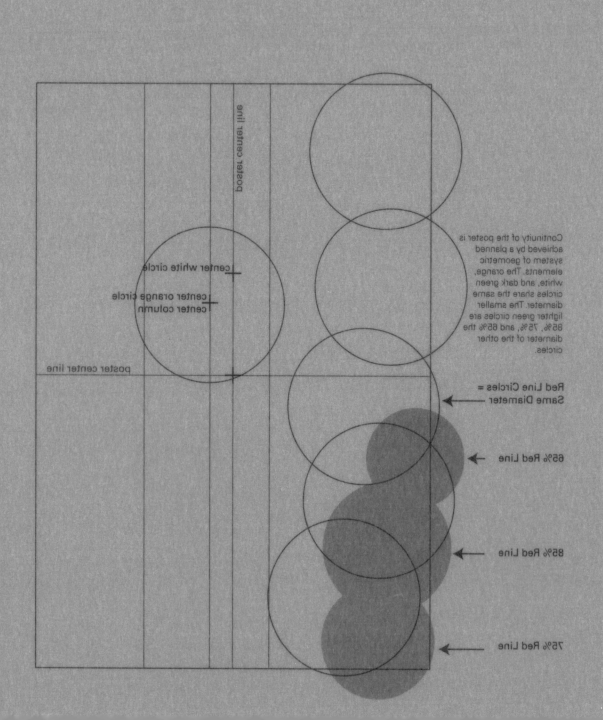

## Bilateral System

Siegfried Odermatt and Rosmarie Tissi have worked as partners since the 1960s and are one of the best-known graphic design studios in Switzerland. Their poster for Serenaden 92 becomes an abstract landscape with an orange setting sun and a white, rising crescent moon. The landscape is further defined by the green "forest" and the text and rules that play down the page like a reflection on water.

The text is arranged in a bilateral column that is slightly offset to the right. Each text group is organized by a red rule to the left and balanced by a similar rule to the right, creating an abstract reflection of light from the sun and moon on water. The ancillary information at the bottom does not employ the right-side rules, so the reflection appears to diminish near the bottom of the page.

Odermatt & Tissi, 1992

It is appropriate that a work discussing "the new discourse" employs an inventive structural variation on the traditional single-column manuscript grid. The bilateral symmetry is beautifully offset by the reflected shifting of space as a single column is divided into two. The names at the top and the title that drops out of black rules provide counterpoint to the symmetry. Key words are threaded between the lines at the axis: Art/science, Mathematic/poetic, Desire/necessity....These words reflect the text discussion of the duality of design.

KATHERINE mcCoy
MICHAEL mcCoy

Art science
Nothing pulls you into the territory between art and science quite so quickly as design. It is the borderline where contradictions and tensions exist between the quantifiable and the poetic. It is the field between desire and necessity. Designers thrive in those conditions, moving between land and water. A typical critique at Cranbrook can easily move in a matter of minutes between
Mathematic poetic
a discussion of the object as a validation of being to the precise mechanical proposal for actuating the object. The discussion moves from Heidegger to the "strange material of the week" or from Lyotard to printing technologies without missing a beat. The free flow of ideas, and the leaps from the technical to the mythical, stem from the attempt to maintain a studio plat-
Desire necessity
form that supports each student's search to find his or her own voice as a designer. The studio is a hothouse that enables students
the and faculty to encounter their own visions of the world and act on them — a
new process that is at times chaotic, conflicting, and occasionally inspiring.

Watching the process of students absorbing new ideas and influences, and the incredible range of in- terpretations of those ideas into design, is
Mythology technology
an annual experience that is always amaz- ing. In recent years, for example, the de-
discourse partment has had the experience of watching wood craftsmen metamorphose into high technologists, and graphic designers into software humanists. Yet it all seems consistent. They are bringing a very personal vision to an area that desperately needs it. The messiness of human experi-
Purist pluralist
ence is warming up the cold precision of technology to make it livable, and lived in.

Unlike the Bauhaus, Cranbrook never embraced a singular teaching method or philosophy, other than Saarinen's exhortation to each student to find his or her own way, in the company of other artists and designers who were engaged in the same search. The energy at Cranbrook seems to come from the fact of
Individual communal
the mutual search, although not the mutual conclusion. If design is about life, why shouldn't it have all the complexity, variety, contradiction, and sublimity of life?

Much of the work done at Cranbrook has been dedicated to changing the status quo. It is polemical, calculated to ruffle designers' feathers. And
Dangerous rigorous

Katherine McCoy, P. Scott Makela, Mary Lou Kroh, 1990

Gail Swanlund's design brings the intensity of a visceral rage to this page from *Emigre* magazine. It is ironic that bilateral alignment, more closely associated with traditional design, is used in a work that discusses the "Information Superhighway." The bilateral arrangement begins with a justified column at the top, shifts to flush left, and then to an irregular arrangement whereby the line breaks echo the phrasing of the text. The fonts seem to have the irregularities of the intonation of human speech and become a visual voice. Softer, then louder, the type speaks and questions as it collides, overlaps, and finally finishes with a blackletter "The end."

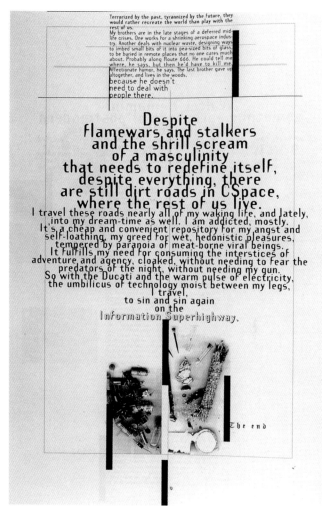

Gail Swanlund, *Emigre* Magazine #32, 1994

# Bilateral System, Thumbnail Variations

There is beauty in symmetry, the hallmark of the bilateral system. However, when working in the system the appreciation of the beauty of symmetry quickly gives way to boredom. Designers rapidly cycle through the expected variations of symmetrical composition and experiment with differing shapes of text blocks; the resulting compositions feel traditional and somewhat static.

Placing the bilateral axis off center opens new venues of composition. Space can be shaped and reorganized with volumes of white space. It is the composition with space that leads to some of the most interesting solutions. This system inspires the designer to seek creativity with the organization of space and the simple elements of line breaks, spacing, and asymmetrical placement of the bilateral axis.

### Initial Phase

Initial work with the system gives the designer an opportunity to explore symmetrical arrangement. Although placement of the axis is centered, leading, line breaks, and alignment are variable.

### Intermediate Phase

Many of the initial compositions can be readily enhanced by placing the bilateral axis off center, resulting in asymmetry. The proportion of the volumes of space changes, making the composition more interesting.

### Advanced Phase

Advanced work explores the creative challenge more fully. Experiments with voluminous negative space, angled lines, and angled axes change the compositional space.

**1.**
Ringling School of Art and Design
Graphic + Interactive Communication Department
Architectonic Graphic Design Free Public Lecture
7:00 pm Keating Hall
February 10, 2006
February 17, 2006
February 24, 2006

**2.**
Ringling School
of Art and Design
Graphic+Interactive
Communication
Department Free
Public Lecture
7:00 pm Keating
Hall Architectonic
Graphic Design
February 10, 2006
February 17, 2006
February 24, 2006

**3.**
Ringling School of Art and Design
Graphic + Interactive Communication Department
Architectonic Graphic Design Free Public Lecture
7:00 pm, Keating Hall, February 10, 2006
February 17, 2006 February 24, 2006

**4.**
Ringling School
of Art and Design
Graphic + Interactive
Communication Department
Architectonic
Graphic
Design
Free Public Lecture
7:00 pm
Keating Hall
February 10, 2006
February 17, 2006
February 24, 2006

**5.**
Architectonic Graphic Design
Ringling School of Art and Design
Graphic + Interactive
Communication Department
Free Public Lecture
7:00 pm
Keating Hall
February 10, 2006
February 17, 2006
February 24, 2006

**6.**
Ringling School
of Art and Design
Graphic & Inter
active Communi
cation Department
Architectonic
Graphic Design
Free Public lecture
7 : 0 0  p m
Keating Hall
February 10, 2006
February 17, 2006
February 24, 2006

**7.**
Ringling School
of Art and Design
Graphic & Interact
ive Communicat
ion Department
Free public lecture
7pm Keating hall
Architectonic
Graphic Design
February 10, 2006
February 17, 2006
February 24, 2006

**8.**
Ringling School of
Art and Design Gra
phic & Interactive
Communication De
partment Free Pub
lic lecture 7:00 pm
Keating Hall Febru
ary 10, 2006 Febru
ary 17, 2006 Febru
ary 24, 2006
Architectonic
Graphic
Design

**9.**
Graphic and interactive communication department
Architectonic Graphic Design
Ringling School of art and design
7:00pm Keating Hall
February 15, 2005
February 22, 2005
Free public lecture

## Symmetry & Tone

All of these works employ a symmetrically placed bilateral axis in compositions that are essentially restricted to type without nonobjective elements. The circle, always a wildcard element, becomes all the more important as it is often the only noncentered element in a structurally symmetrical composition.

All of the examples on this spread are symmetrical compositions with exactly the same text, but each is highly individualized through line placement, line breaks, and the use of tone. The work to the right uses full lines of text and punctuates the symmetry with changes in tone that are also hierarchical guides as they order the message.

An early composition below left uses tone in alternate lines of type. The later composition, below right, employs a more selective hierarchy and only emphasizes a few words for a more asymmetric effect.

Dustin Blouse

Christian Andersen

Christian Andersen

## Symmetry & Tone

Sporadic changes in the tone of lines and individual characters create variety in the composition to the right. Tone changes are spontaneous and provide a textural play in space. The two floating lines are emphasized by their single tones and isolated placement. Below right, slightly angled lines unsettle the symmetry and create tensions as lines overlap. Interestingly, one line of type is turned upside down as a point of contrast.

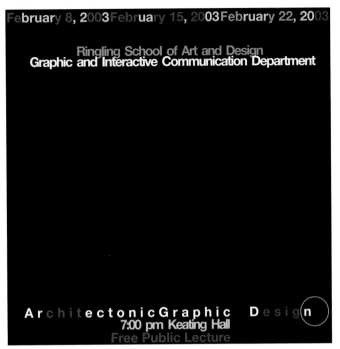

Giselle Guerrero

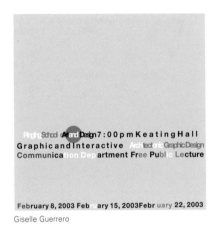

Giselle Guerrero

Early study for the composition above right.

Jonathon Seniw

## Nonobjective Elements

The introduction of nonobjective elements to the bilateral system can enhance symmetry and create visual interest. The tight text group in the composition to the right seems to be balanced on a very thin vertical line, and the black circle becomes an asymmetric accent element. Groups of text are differentiated through changes in spacing, which adds variety to the texture. Below the red rules emphasize the titles and anchor the compositions by spanning the width of the format and bleeding off the edges. The hairline square below right encloses the text group and relates it strongly to the title as the line meets the heavy red rule.

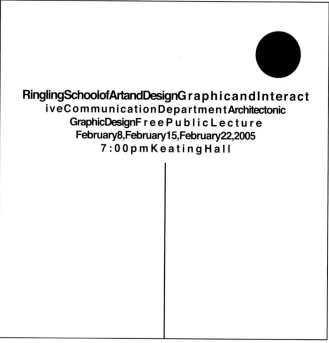

Christian Andersen

Jennifer Levreault

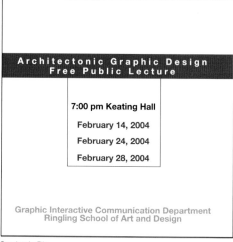

Stephanie Flis

## Nonobjective Elements

The black square within the square format to the right tightly encloses the text. Lines are all uppercase and run the full width of the square without word spacing. Words are broken irregularly as they meet the edge and important words are slightly larger and set off with a gray tone. A similar strategy in the composition below right is used as a circle surrounds a text group. Here the text bleeds off of the edges of the circle into the background. Below left, the step-stairs blocks become forceful elements of enclosure.

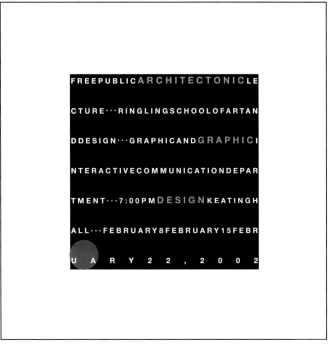

Gray West

Loni Diep

Loni Diep

## Asymmetric Nonobjective

All of the type compositions on this
spread are strictly symmetrical in the
format, but the nonobjective elements
give them asymmetry. The two works
are very simple bilateral type compositions, and they benefit from a gray rule
that extends from the left edge. This
rule not only creates asymmetry but
also creates a hierarchy by emphasizing
the title of the presentation.

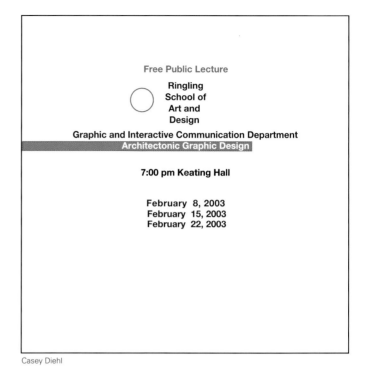

Casey Diehl

Casey Diehl

Early study for the compositions.

Casey Diehl

150

**Asymmetric Nonobjective**

In contrast to the simplicity of the works on the previous page, these compositions use the visual force of large nonobjective elements to create asymmetry. Circles invade the space in all three and feel even larger because they are cropped off the edge of the format.

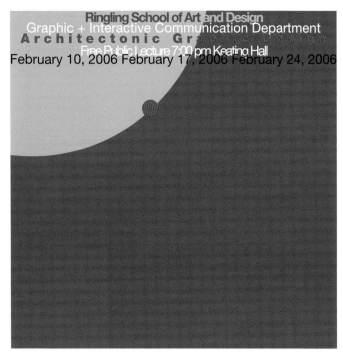

Amanda Clark

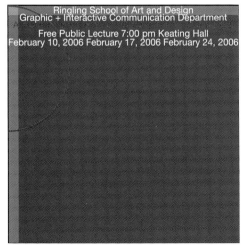

Amanda Clark

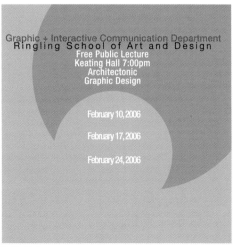

Phillip Clark

## Asymmetric Placement

All of these works employ an asymmetrically placed bilateral axis in compositions that are essentially restricted to type without nonobjective elements. This increases interest because the spaces left and right of the bilateral composition are unequal, and the eye engages in the change in proportion and the shapes created. These examples involve only minimal nonobjective elements, yet the compositions are compelling.

Dustin Blouse

Trish Tatman

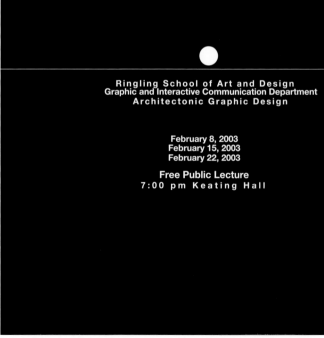

Pushpita Saha

Casey McCauley

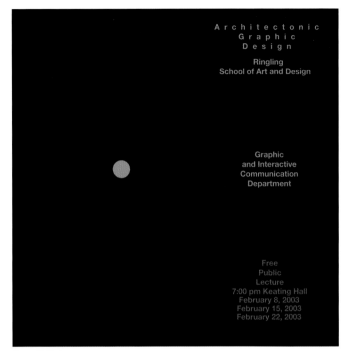

Casey McCauley

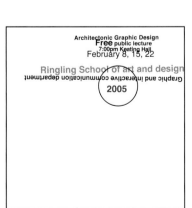

Jonathon Seniw

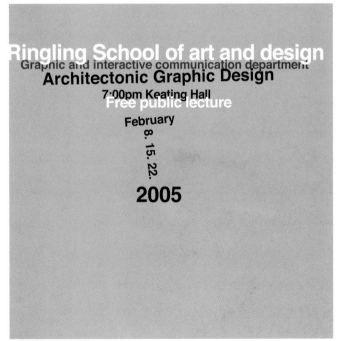

Jonathon Seniw

## Asymmetric Placement

All of these compositions have both an asymmetrically placed bilateral axis and a large nonobjective element. The non-objective circle and rectangle seem to encroach upon the compositional space from the corner. Corner placement and cropping allude to movement and make the element appear larger since the eye completes the unseen portion of the object.

In all cases the type is subordinated to the scale and tone of the nonobjective element. Heightened visual interest in the composition as a whole balances the shift in emphasis from the type to the shape.

Monique Hotard

Wendy Ellen Gingerich

Study in one size, one weight for the nonobjective composition to the right.

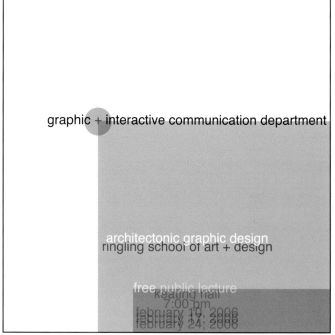

Wendy Ellen Gingerich

## Bilateral System

Loni Diep

Study in one size, one weight for the nonobjective composition to the right.

Loni Diep

Pushpita Saha

Study in one size, one weight for the nonobjective composition to the right.

Pushpita Saha

## Acknowledgments

A very special thanks to my students from the Ringling School of Art and Design who have contributed work, and transformed my teaching from a process of indoctrination to a partnership of creative inquiry.

Thanks to Mona Bagla, Elizabeth Centolella, and Chris Haslup for research and administrative assistance. A special thanks to the Ringling School of Art and Design, Faculty and Staff Development Grant Committee, for supporting this project.

## Image Credits

## Selected Bibliography

Apeloig, Philippe. *Inside the Word*. Switzerland: Lars Mül-ler Publishers, 2001

Blackwell, Lewis. *20th-Century Type*. New Haven: Yale University Press, 2004.

Blackwell, Lewis. *20th Century Type: Remix*. Corte Madera, CA: Gingko Press Inc., 1998.

Blackwell, Lewis and David Carson. *David Carson: 2ndsight: Grafik design after the end of print*. New York: Universe Publishing, 1997

Broos, Kees. and Paul Hefting, *A Century of Dutch Graphic Design*. Cambridge: MIT Press, 1993.

Cohen, Arthur A. *Herbert Bayer*. Cambridge: MIT Press, 1984.

Davis, Susan E. *Typography 23: Annual of the Type Direc-tors Club*. New York: HBI, 2002.

Elam, Kimberly. *Expressive Typography: The Word as Image*. New York: Van Nostrand Reinhold, 1990.

Elam, Kimberly. *Geometry of Design: Studies in Propor-tion and Composition*. New York: Princeton Architectural Press, 2001.

Elam, Kimberly. *Grid Systems: Principles of Organizing Type*. New York: Princeton Architectural Press, 2004.

Friedl, Friedrich, Nicolaus Ott, and Bernard Stein. *Typography: An encyclopedic survey of type design and techniques throughout history*. New York: Black Dog and Leventhal Publishers, Inc., 1998.

Gottschall, Edward M. *Typographic Communication Today*. Cambridge: MIT Press, 1989.

Harper, Laurel. *Radical graphics/graphic radicals*. San Francisco. Chronicle Books, 1999.

Küsters, Christian, and Emily King. *Restart: New Systems in Graphic Design*. New York: Universe Publishing, 2001.

Lupton, Ellen. *Thinking with Type: A Critical Guide for Designers, Writers, Editors, and Students*. New York: Princeton Architectural Press, 2004.

McCoy, Katherine, P. Scott Makela, and Mary Lou Kroh. *Cranbrook Design: the new discourse*. New York: Rizzoli International, Inc., 1990.

Meggs, Philip B. *The History of Graphic Design: 3rd Ed*. New York: John Wiley and Sons, Inc., 1998.

Meggs, Philip B. *Type & Image: The Language of Graphic Design*. New York: Van Nostrand Reinhold, 1989.

Müller-Brockmann, Josef. *Grid Systems in Graphic Design*. Switzerland: Arthur Niggli Ltd., 1981.

Poynor, Rick. *No More Rules: Graphic Design and Post-modernism*. New Haven: Yale University Press, 2003.

Poynor, Rick, and Edward Booth-Clibborn and Why Not Associates. *Typography Now: The Next Wave*. Japan: Dai Nippon, 1991.

Poynor, Rick. *Typography Now Two Implosion*. London: Booth-Clibborn Editions, 1996.

Rüegg, Ruedi, and Godi Fröhlich. *Basic Typography: Hand-book of technique and design*. Zurich: ABC Verlag, 1972.

Ruder, Emil. *Typography: A Manual of Design*. Switzer-land: Arthur Niggli ltd., 1967.

Samara, Timothy. *Making and Breaking the Grid: A Graphic Design Layout Workshop*. Gloucester, MA: Rock-port Publishers, 2002.

Schmid, Helmut. *Typography Today*. Tokyo: Seibundo Shinkosha, 1980.

Skolos, Nancy, and Thomas Wedell. *Type Image Mes-sage: A Graphic Design Layout Workshop*. Gloucester, MA: Rockport Publishers, 2006.

Spencer, Herbert. *Pioneers of Modern Typography*. Cam-bridge: MIT Press, 1983.

Vignelli, Massimo. *Design: Vignelli*. New York: Rizzoli International Publications, Inc., 1990.

Walton, Roger. *Typographics 3*. New York: Harper Design International, 2000.

Walton, Roger. *Typographics 4*. New York: Harper Design International, 2004.

# Index